CU00820155

DANCING MY DREAM

Warren Petoskey

Odawa-Lakotah

"Warren Petoskey's work, the telling of his personal story, is an attempt to break the cycle of pain and dysfunction. The revelation of his own pain and suffering will encourage other native people to come forward, and hopefully, non-native people will gain a measure of understanding, which will result in a more human approach in dealing with Indians."

— *Dr. Kay McGowan, Choctaw-Cherokee anthropologist*

"In my 75 years, I have read countless autobiographies and spiritual works. Warren Petoskey's uplifting memoir ranks among the best. *Dancing My Dream* is written simply, flowingly and lovingly, by a man of immense dignity and hard-won spirituality. It meshes the Native American with the Christian. It is for believers and nonbelievers, for those of any religion or none. It is a basic Book of Existence; reading it is like ingesting the food of life."

— *Javan Kienzle, author of "Judged By Love"*

"Warren's inner peace is palpable and rubs off, like the Dalai Lama's. He may not be as well known and he doesn't claim to be a shaman, but I personally have no doubt that he possesses the gift of healing. He struggled to heal his own spirit over many years, and is now able to help heal the spirits of others."

— *Patricia Chargot, journalist and author of "Balto: the Untold Story of Alaska's Famous Iditarod Sled Dog"*

DANCING MY DREAM

Warren Petoskey
Odawa-Lakotah

For ongoing discussion and additional material, visit
www.DancingMyDream.info

You may contact the author via the publisher:
ReadTheSpirit@gmail.com

Cover art and design by
Rick Nease
www.RickNease.com

Published by
Read The Spirit Books, an imprint of
David Crumm Media, LLC
42015 Ford Rd., Suite 234
Canton, Michigan 48187
U.S.A.

For information about customized editions, bulk purchases or
permissions, contact David Crumm Media, LLC at
info@DavidCrummMedia.com
734-786-3815

Dedication

*I*n honor of the victims and survivors of the Indian boarding schools, orphanages and foster care systems we experienced on Turtle Island.

Contents

Dedication v

Acknowledgments vii

Foreward ix

A Note from the Editor xiii

A New Day 1

Walking the Red Road 5

The Early Road 11

Dancing My Dream 21

Affirmation 25

Negation 31

My People 35

Entering the Circle 39

Sunset One 45

Sunset Two 47

Morning Prayer of an Odawa 49

Fishing 51

Mother Earth 57

Loss 65

Hunting 71

My Heart Attack 77

Brave Native Women 87

Walk in Grace 91

Wedded Prejudice 97

Barbara's Story 101

Come Follow Me 111

Peace Is 117

All Things Beautiful 119

The Source 121

Dad Walks On 127

The City of Petoskey 131

Making Music 135

About the Author 141

Acknowledgments

I would like to acknowledge all those who have influenced me and contributed to my life. I cannot begin to name them all because there are so many. I am rich in friends and you know who you are.

I want to first acknowledge my wife, Barbara Louise Curton Petoskey. You came to me as a gift from the Creator, and brought a greater consciousness and understanding of who He is. We have danced the dream together all these years, and I believe, my Love, that the best is yet to come. Thank you for your love and commitment to me and the children you blessed me with. I want to acknowledge our seven children and 14 grandchildren, who have brought so much joy and excitement to our lives.

I want to acknowledge my father and mother, Warren Frank and Juanita Mae Petoskey—my mother for her devotion and encouragement through the years, and my father for his recovery and effort to be the father I needed; my brother, Jon; and my sisters, Juanita June and Ella Rose, who have put up with me all their lives as their older brother.

I want to acknowledge my grandfathers: Clyde Howlett, who spent so much time teaching me about honor and the work ethic but also about how to have fun; and Cornelius Joseph Petoskey, whom I never got to know, but who, through his experiences at Carlisle Industrial School, led me to healing and recovery from the residuals those experiences deposited in my life.

I want to acknowledge George and Carolyn White, Bishop L.A. Parent and William Parent, Bishop Roland Baker and all of our Tribal Elders; in particular Ella Jane Petoskey, Simon Otto, Ted Holappa, Edward Wilson and Joseph Mitchell, all of whom have spent a lot of time teaching me and praying for me.

I want to acknowledge all my friends at Life Tabernacle in Gaylord, Michigan, especially Jim and Char Wickson and Jim and Lisa Tobin.

I want to acknowledge David Crumm, Pat Chargot, Javan Kienzle and Stephanie Fenton for their editing contributions and suggestions, without which this book would never have come to live. I can never say enough to express my gratitude for your dedication and vision regarding this effort.

Most of all I want to acknowledge the Great God, the Creator, who manifested Himself to us as Jesus Christ. He came to me when I was a boy, led me to my wife, protected me through major depression and brought me to the place where I was finally able to see some value in myself. He taught me in dreams and through His Book that, as an Indian, I have an origin and a destination: because of this understanding I also have a purpose.

Foreward

The Indian Boarding School story that Warren Petoskey shares with readers is all too familiar to Indians in the United States and Canada. The story, however, is an unfamiliar one to white America. It is a story that needs to be told.

Virtually every Indian family was touched by the policy of assimilation that the boarding schools were designed to promote. "Kill the Indian, but save the child" was the desired outcome. Instead of assimilation, the boarding schools created a syndrome of intergenerational trauma that affects most Indians in America to this day.

A 4-year-old or 6-year-old-child, taken from a loving family and put into a military-style living situation, had a very difficult time growing up to be a loving, caring parent or spouse.

The breakdown in the Indian family was enormously destructive, resulting in high rates of alcoholism, mental illness and suicide; it was a direct effect of the failed Indian boarding school system.

Survivors of the boarding schools have a high tolerance for trauma because it was a way of life in their formative years; violence became a "normal" experience. The sheer brutality of taking young children from their families has left a deep wound in Indian country.

Because of their high level of tolerance for trauma and deviance, victims of boarding school syndrome are likely to be re-victimized in their lifetime—sometimes many times over. Generation after generation felt the effect of the boarding schools, as Warren Petoskey's experience shows.

In addition to the intergenerational trauma created by the boarding schools, Indian history is marked with diseases, massacres, warfare, slaughter, slavery, relocation to reservations, gender violence, colonization, urban relocation and forced sterilization of native women, as recently as the 1970s. Outlawing the practice of traditional religious beliefs and practices and placing Indian children in non-Indian adoptive and foster homes has created a combined rage and unresolved grief that staggers the mind and spirit. The boarding schools are just one of many injustices Native Americans have faced in their own land.

Warren Petoskey's work—the telling of his personal story—is an attempt to put the issue on the table; to break the cycle of pain and dysfunction. The revelation of his own pain and suffering will encourage other native people to come forward and hopefully, non-native people will gain a measure of understanding, which will result in a more human approach in dealing with Indians.

The failure of U.S. Indian policy demonstrates that a government cannot manipulate an entire population, giving people no voice in their treatment, and then demanding that they accept "their fate." Native people have been deeply hurt and damaged by the decisions of our government. The boarding schools were penal institutions. Many children were farmed out and became "free child labor" for white farmers. There was a high death rate as children succumbed as a result of epidemic illness and depression; girls were impregnated by their caretakers and murdered. In many cases, families were not even notified of their child's death.

The ethnocentric boarding school period was the result of mainstream society's devaluation of traditional knowledge and education, of feeling they had nothing to learn from Indians. This was the epitome of arrogance.

The assault on Indian children was not only an assault on their bodies, but also on their language, religion, lifeways and even physical appearance. It was an assault on the Indian family and on Indian culture, on a complete way of life that the United States hoped to destroy.

Warren Petoskey has come to grips with his own life and experiences. He says his spirit is calmed and his heart softened. His words will help other Indians achieve what he has achieved. His words are prayers for Indian people: prayers of hopefulness against all odds.

The degradation of our Mother the Earth mirrors the degradation of the Indian people. A lack of respect for both the environment and Indian people is reflected in the pollution and other environmental abuse that Warren Petoskey describes. To the materialistic, nothing is sacred except money, but all of us will suffer from their actions and lack of concern for the earth, air and water.

Warren's greatest triumph has been forgiving his father for the abuse that was inflicted on him as a young boy. Warren came to understand his father's anger and, in his final days, he and his father found love and peace with each another. Many native people are not so fortunate.

I join the chorus of native scholars in calling for the establishment of a truth commission in the United States to relieve the suffering of native peoples. My own grandmother was at the Carlisle Boarding School with Warren Petoskey's grandfather. None of us are untouched.

—*Kay McGowan, Choctaw-Cherokee anthropologist*

Dr. McGowan is a Michigan anthropologist who has taught classes on the native cultures of North America at several colleges and universities in the Midwest. She has testified before the United Nations on issues related to indigenous peoples.

A Note from the Editor

As a journalist interested in indigenous cultures, it has been my privilege to have interviewed native people from more than three dozen tribes in the United States, Mexico and Canada.

More often than not, the interviews ended with a simple, heartfelt request:

"We're still here! Please tell your readers that. Most people think we died out with the buffalo."

Initially, I was taken aback, failing to grasp the profound grief and sense of loss inherent in such comments. The existence of 21st century Native Americans seemed self-evident as the warp, or foundation, of our diverse cultural fabric—whose weft was woven much later, by the Europeans and other immigrants.

Sadly, it's not self-evident. With so little news coverage of native affairs beyond casinos—and Native Americans comprising only 1.5 percent of the U.S. population—it's easy to conclude that native people virtually have ceased to walk among us.

We see their beautiful artwork and historic artifacts in museums, and we gaze wonderingly at the dignified countenances in those old photographs in the New York

Times that the paper runs to boost reprint sales for its photo archives.

But the truth is that most non-native Americans have never met a "real Indian."—or they don't think they have, anyway, because Indians of mixed ancestry are often hard to spot and tribal members only wear their colorful regalia for powwows. Native Americans also keep a low profile: They are still targets of discrimination, more than 500 years after Columbus landed.

So it gives me great pleasure to introduce a Native American who is very much alive and walking, talking, hunting and fishing among us—my dear friend, spiritual teacher and email and camping buddy, Warren Petoskey.

Warren, 63, lives in Michigan's Upper Peninsula and is Waganakising Odawa, an Elder of the Little Traverse Bay Band of Odawas.

His traditional name is Biidassige, which means "One Who Brings the Light." The name belonged to his great-great-grandfather, Ignatius Petoskey, and it has taken him awhile to live up to it, as he so candidly tells readers in *Dancing My Dream*.

But he has lived up to his name, and Warren has since brought light into the lives of countless people, especially survivors of the infamous U.S. Indian boarding school system and those suffering from addictions.

As the editor of Warren's book, it has been my good fortune to step into that circle of light, too. So have many other non-native Americans, including my good friend and sister journalist, Javan Kienzle, who also worked on Warren's book—and loves it as much as I do.

Warren's light just keeps growing brighter and brighter as more and more people in Michigan—and across the country—gravitate to his lectures; now people can also read his book and listen to the music on his first CD.

He has the heart of a warrior, and those who underestimate Indians or treat them badly might want to steer clear. But his spirituality is readily apparent to those receptive to it, and to be in his presence—or even communicate with him by email, as I did regularly for so long—is to come away feeling lighter, happier and more centered. It takes a very special person to have that kind of effect on people.

Warren's inner peace is palpable and rubs off, like the Dalai Lama's. He may not be as well known and he doesn't claim to be a shaman, but I personally have no doubt that he possesses the gift of healing. He struggled to heal his own spirit over many years, and is now able to help heal the spirits of others.

A year and a half ago, I'd never heard of Warren Petoskey—and I had no idea that the northern Michigan resort town of Petoskey, which I'd visited many times since childhood, was named after his great-great-grandfather Ignatius. How could I not have known? My own ignorance speaks reams about the invisibility of Native Americans.

Warren is a treasure, a living link to the time before European settlement: A time when Michigan was an uncut primeval forest, and native people plied the pristine waters of the Great Lakes in birch bark canoes to catch untainted fish and make their way to and from their winter hunting grounds and summer villages.

Warren's ancestors traveled across Lake Michigan to what today is Wisconsin and Minnesota, returning in spring to the northwest corner of what is now Michigan's Lower Peninsula.

Deer didn't have chronic wasting disease when Warren's ancestors inhabited this land, and there were no syringes or other litter along the beaches. In the villages, children never encountered toxic toys, ruined their teeth with sugar or grew obese on junk food.

In his book, Warren paints a picture of a time that non-native readers will never forget and may even realize they long for—as Warren does every single day. As my dear friend Kay McGowan, a Native American anthropologist, likes to say, "We're all descended from indigenous people, some of us much more recently than others."

What have we lost and how can we get it back? Warren knows—it's written in his genetic code—and has some important answers for all of us.

For me, 2008 was the "Year of Warren;" a very special time that has come to an end, as good things always do. Starting in January and for the next nine months, I helped him put together his memoirs from a huge pile of essays, poems and speeches. We emailed daily, and sometimes many times per day.

Initially, Warren sent a much smaller bundle of his writings to ReadTheSpirit Editor David Crumm, who passed it along to me. Then the pile started growing, as Warren sent another essay and another and another, even writing new essays on subjects that I thought would be of interest to readers, such as his hunting and fishing adventures. (One of my favorite chapters is "Fishing": in particular, I enjoyed the section on ice fishing in sub-zero temperatures in the UP. Anyone who likes to eat whitefish will want to read this chapter. Hemingway surely would, if he were alive.)

Warren would send me an email with a tantalizing tidbit, and I'd shoot back: "Warren, why don't you write about that?" And he would, banging out new material as quickly and cleanly as a professional journalist on deadline.

Warren writes from the heart, from a place deeper inside himself than even his childhood. In some sections, he speaks for his ancestors—perhaps they even speak through him—of a lost way life that he is trying to reclaim, by living close to nature and ignoring the more dehumanizing aspects and ills of modernism and capitalism.

I admire Warren, and would like to live more like he does: listening to more silence and less noise; greeting the morning sun and talking to the Creator and reveling in the gifts of creation that surround us still, if we choose to see them and pay attention.

The humility and guilelessness with which Warren speaks of the Creator—the Native Americans' term for God—is an inspiration. He never flaunts his connection with the

Creator, like so many Christians and others seem to do these days—hitting you on the head with their born-again fervor and assaulting even strangers with "What Would Jesus Do?" bumper stickers and pins.

I hate that stuff.

By comparison, Warren's connection with the Creator seems so much more authentic. The term "Creator" rolls from his lips so naturally that I've come to prefer it myself—and I'm Catholic.

Through hundreds of emails from Warren—mostly related to the book, yet all of them personal and some of them very personal—my own connection to the Creator has been strengthened. I have become less inhibited at prayer and more open to intimacy of a sort that I think many believers—and even doubters—are struggling toward right now.

We want to connect! We don't want priests and other clergy to always be our intermediaries. We want what Warren has: absolute trust and faith in God.

Once, Warren shared a dream in an email. I believe every word of it, and reading that email felt like the equivalent of seeing a unicorn in the forest.

The email began with, "Sounds great," a reference to a minor change I had made in a chapter for the book. It then segued into, "I have to tell you about a dream I had probably 10 years ago.

> I was standing on a bluff, overlooking the Great Lake early in the morning; I was waiting for the sun to appear, so that I could offer my prayers. When the sun appeared on the horizon, I held my semma (sacred tobacco) above my head, pointing it toward the sun. There was a spot on the sun, and I became focused on this spot that began to grow larger in my sight.
>
> After a few moments, I could tell that the spot was a gold eagle encased in flames, but not consumed. When they were visible, the eagle's eyes were fixed on me. I felt apprehensive, but not afraid. I wanted to fall to the

ground, but could not; It seemed that I was frozen to the spot. The eagle hit me in the chest, but I was not injured. I turned to watch the rest of his flight, but he was not to be seen. I took it that the golden eagle was a messenger sent from the Creator. I have not told this to many people, but when I read your idea about the photo of the lakeshore at the Dunes, the memory of that dream came back to me ...

I'm still pinching myself with the thought that I was the recipient of such emails, and am deeply grateful to know that Warren continues to pray for me and hold me in his heart. I'll keep them always and reread them, including these words of encouragement that Warren sent last fall, after I gave up my longtime reporter's job at the Detroit Free Press and told him—in an email—that I was feeling a little lost:

"It is a new day for you," he wrote.

"You have lived in the environment that developed around you over the past 37 years; that environment no longer exists. You are not the environment and the environment is not you. You are a free, moral agent on a journey from a sacred beginning. You are the daughter of the Creator of all things and His nature is in you. We recreate our lives over and over again through our physical experience. You are the greatest asset you have.

"Sometimes we have to just rest where we are and wait for the next door to open. It is said that when we open the door of our understanding, the messengers will come. It took courage to make the decision you did, but it was not an accident, nor a spur-of-the-moment decision. The path will become clearer for you soon."

I still get tears in my eyes when I read those lines, and I just did again. Warren gives me strength. I love the guy.

I'll leave our camping adventure for another time: I want to write about it at length because it was a very special experience that I'd like share with readers of ReadTheSpirit (http://www.ReadTheSpirit.com).

In the meantime, I strongly urge you to buy Warren's book. It's the story of one Native American's suffering and redemption after decades of pain, confusion and self-destruction.

Yet Warren't book is filled with hope—and so much light it should come packaged with sunglasses!

The best possible place to read it, I think, would be outdoors, under a tree.

Warren is "Walking the Red Road," and beckons us to follow. As he writes, the red road is "a consciousness" that's accessible to us all:

"I welcome everyone to come and share this journey with me. ... It is a good path to travel."

—*Patricia Chargot*

Note: For those interested in learning more about Native American spirituality, a good place to start is *God Is Red, a Native View of Religion,* by Vine Deloria Jr. Named by Time magazine as one of the greatest religious thinkers of the 20th Century, Deloria died in 2005, two years after a special 30th anniversary edition of his seminal work was issued.

A New Day

My English name is Warren Donald Petoskey. I am an Elder with the Odawa and Lakotah Nations. My lovely wife, Barbara Louise Curton Petoskey, is Cherokee and Choctaw. I was born in Michigan and Barbara was born in Missouri.

My wife's relatives were in the long walk from Georgia to the Indian Territory. In the 1830s, the entire Cherokee Nation—about 17,000 people—was driven from its homeland and forced to migrate to what today is Oklahoma. Thousands of men, women and children died along the way.

Together, Barbara and I bring a lot of baggage in blood memory of the tragic histories surrounding our peoples.

Living in a world that presented things as true that I knew were untrue, I asked the Giver of Life to teach me the truth as He meant it to be, because I had read that truth would set one free.

The Creator gave me a dream, showing me the Path of Life and His promise of a successful journey if I followed His directions. In another dream He showed me the woman I would share my life with and, seven years later, we met and married. We have seven children and 14 grandchildren.

For more than a decade, I have counseled many of those suffering the residual effects of the historical trauma created by the nation's infamous Indian boarding school system.

From the 1880s to 1983, when the last school closed, the U.S. government sent an estimated 100,000 children to the schools, often for years, in a cruel attempt to "Kill the Indian, save the human." My father, Warren Frank Petoskey, was one of those children. So was my grandfather, Cornelius Joseph Petoskey.

Those who tried to speak their native language or practice their spiritual traditions were beaten. It was not until 1978 that the U.S. Congress gave us back our right to worship in our own way.

We, Indian people—those of us alive today—have survived five centuries of near-constant assassination and extermination attempts. We have survived genocide, chemical and germ warfare, terrorism, sterilization, relocation, reservations, urbanization, boarding schools, orphanages and the foster care system, all of which were designed to erase the consciousness of what it means to be an Indian in North America. Our hearts have been on the ground because of all these things.

We still exhibit high rates of suicide, spousal and child abuse, crime, diabetes and alcohol and drug abuse: indicators of the ongoing, cumulative impact of our grief and loss. I believe that we are here today not because of the benevolence of a controlling government, but because the Creator has willed it to be so.

We know what it is to feel hopeless and to live in fear. We know what it is to be poor and destitute. We know what it is to be unable to feel self-worth, self-esteem or confidence. At one time I lived this kind of life.

But in a moment of desperation I met the Giver of Life, Who took away all these things and filled me with His Spirit. He wanted me to know I was of value to Him. He wanted me to know that He had a better way to live than I knew. He wanted me to know that despite all of the conditions around me, there was hope and the promise of a better life.

Now that the Path to that better life is clear, I want to encourage everyone I can to walk it with me. I long for the home that exists in the Presence of the Great Creator and I try to live my life in a way that will make Him happy; He that gave me life and has shown me the way.

He directed me to write this book out of love and honor for humanity, but especially for my Red Brothers and Sisters, and most especially for the generation that is coming. This coming generation who, I worry, feels no responsibility for the words of their great-grandfathers and great-grandmothers.

I have also written this book to validate our experience as Native Indigenous People. For too long, we have remained silent and have internalized these things.

It is our belief that the Creator has brought us all to this threshold to do the work of healing and recovery: not just of the native race, but of all races. We are spirits in these physical space suits, traveling through time in our journey to return to the Great Sprit. It is an honor to be counted worthy to do what I am doing.

I welcome everyone to come and share this journey with me. We all come from a spiritual origin and we are on our way to a spiritual destination. I can hardly wait to see what is beyond this veil. I am walking the Red Road. It is a good path to travel.

Walking the
Red Road

To the native people of Turtle Island (our name for North America), "Walking the Red Road" is an expression of our commitment to the teachings and beliefs of our ancestors. I am sure that many indigenous peoples in other parts of the world have similar expressions that are as all-encompassing.

I have been asked several times to define what "Walking the Red Road" means to me. It is a deep subject that I believe deserves a thoughtful answer. But I do not believe it can be conveyed in just a few moments of conversation, so I have decided to put my thoughts on paper.

I am an Odawa and Lakotah Tribal Elder. I capitalize these words because they mean so much to me. I am the son, grandson and great-grandson of men and women who tried to live the meaning of the Red Road or were trying to find their way back to it.

Walking the Red Road is a consciousness. It is more than ritual and ceremony, because without consciousness, ritual and ceremony have no meaning.

Many Native Americans practice ritual and ceremony in an attempt to reconnect to their traditions, but miss the essence of it all.

As Native Americans, we need to know how we became disconnected. We need to know how all that has happened to us created a toxicity that damaged—and continues to damage—our spirits, because so many of us have not yet begun to heal and recover.

Before the arrival of the Europeans, we, as Indian people, lived our worship, which made Walking the Red Road easy. Our ceremonies and songs were energized by a consciousness and understanding of our mystical connection to life and to all living things.

Some may take exception to my use of the term "Indian," believing its origin is rooted in Columbus getting lost in his search for India. But India did not exist at that time, and what is now India was then called Hindustan. Columbus was merely an Italian trying to write in Spanish. When he first met the Taino people of the Caribbean, he wrote in his ship log, *"Una gente in Dios,"* which means "a people of God." It is my belief that this entry was made as a result of Columbus' observations and experiences in encountering our ancestors.

We, as Native American people, believe in the prophecies of the Seven Generations. What we fail to understand is that we are the product of the seven generations that preceded us and will affect the seven generations that come after us—if the Creator allows human life to continue for that long—by how we conduct our lives.

All of us—red, yellow, black and white—at one time came from a tribe. But many of us have lost our consciousness of—and connection with—the Creator's Original Intent, because we are more than seven generations removed from those relatives who knew and lived this way of life. We search and struggle through the impediments of a world that prevents our re-discovery of this good way of life.

By Original Intent, I mean our original human consciousness and understanding of Creation: not our creation myths, but the innate understanding that lies buried in our subconscious. When allowed, these myths can surface in thought or consciousness and propel us in a direction opposite from what we have been taught and, in some cases, forced to conform to. I have said that the greatest tragedy is not the loss of one's freedom, but the loss of the knowledge of what true freedom really is.

In the Creator's Original Intent, we were instructed to be caretakers of the garden we were placed in. We believed that everything that was gifted to us came from a benevolent Creator who had our best interests at heart. We didn't think that we owned anything. Living in the world as it was then, there was no fear or danger. There was no stress or anxiety. There was no sickness or disease. I personally believe that even the temperatures were consistent day and night in support of continuing life, and that there was no bitter cold or unbearable heat. There certainly was no pollution, and they who lived this Original Intent would never have thought of abusing themselves, their families or their environment.

We lived this way on Turtle Island for thousands of years before the arrival of the Europeans, their philosophy of Manifest Destiny and their efforts to colonize and populate the continent for profit. In the last 300 years, that philosophy has polluted every corner of our environment and atmosphere. This is additional evidence of our profoundly sad loss of consciousness of Original Intent.

Materialism has done more to damn humanity than just about anything else.

So Walking the Red Road is a consciousness. Walking the Red Road is more than drums, sacred pipes, sweat lodges and traditional medicine. It is a consciousness that gives true meaning to the Medicine Wheel—the Indian symbol for the wheel of life—that is always evolving and bringing new truths to our Earthwalk. It is more than an artistic expression; the flute players, drummers, singers, sweat lodge guides and medicine people who inspire us the most are those who have, themselves, reconnected to that consciousness.

Honesty is the first value that has to be cultivated to recover what has been lost. Each of us needs to go deep inside and identify the conditions that prevent us from progressing.

Where does the rage and anger come from? Where does the sense of alienation and hopelessness come from? Where does the cynicism and distrust come from? Why are we confused and why do we feel so separated from one other? We are the Red Race and, at one time, we loved one another and dwelt in peace. We need to return to the perpetrators those things that were imposed upon our lives, and to realize that they do not belong to us. We need to stop being victims and start being our own advocates for healing and recovery.

We need to hold in our consciousness the knowledge that if we go back seven generations in our families, we go back to a time before the Europeans arrived—a time when our relatives lived the Original Intent. Their blood flows through our veins, as does the blood of each successive generation before our own spirits' sounding on Mother Earth.

We once knew that we were beings from a spiritual origin on our way to a spiritual destination: We lived our lives under this influence. Now, among many of us, this world is all we are conscious of and know. There is no way that consciousness alone can bring balance, harmony and a sense of being centered to our lives.

Walking the Red Road is a journey from our spiritual origin through this world and our physical experience of it, trusting absolutely that the road will lead us again into the Presence of the Great Creator.

Walking the Red Road is walking in consciousness of the presence of the Creator at all times. Walking the Red Road encourages prayer, thankfulness and giving back. Walking the Red Road is a consciousness of our sacred connection to life and all living things, especially of our connection with the Great Creator and His purpose for our existence here. We, as human beings, can be His emissaries or we can be defiant and be perpetrators of conditions contrary to a respect for all life.

We are scattered as a people, not just in a geographical sense but in our consciousness. We need to come together again as one people comprising many individual tribes, so we can counter the conditions that created the dysfunction and trauma among us. If we come together, we will see the changes these efforts will bring to our children and grandchildren for seven generations to come—and beyond. We can all find our way through the chaos of Western culture and through the wilderness that has been created by its callousness and unconscionable conduct. We all know the way home. It is in us all to Walk the Red Road.

The Early Road

My mother was visiting her grandmother when she went into labor. I was born at Mercy Hospital in Jackson, Michigan, on June 3, 1945, a little after 3 a.m.

My father was overseas in the service, so my mother and I lived in her apartment in Lansing. When my father came home in 1946, we moved to Harrison, in northern Michigan. Of course I have no recollection of this time, but it is what I have been told.

In 1949, my father was offered the village engineer's position in Stockbridge, downstate, and we moved into an apartment owned by my mother's grandfather.

My brother, Jon, was a year-and-a-half younger than I; we were wanderers. Dad put up a snow fence in the backyard to try to corral us, but we scaled the fence.

In the old way, it was important to teach young boys to hunt and fish. Dad and Grandpa started Jon and I early, and we enjoyed the hours in the boat and on the ice, fishing; hunting was another thing. Neither my brother nor I was old enough to carry a gun, and so we usually got left behind, except for an occasional rabbit hunt with Dad. We didn't have a dog, but that didn't matter: Dad had a way of tracking a rabbit right to the brush pile he was hiding under.

I remember kindergarten in the basement of the Presbyterian church; I hated the sleeping mats and forced naps. During the summer, I spent every daylight hour in the woods or at the lakes around Stockbridge, stealing out of my bedroom window before first light and staying away until dark. I made a fishing pole out of a long stick and what monofilament I could scrounge, but Dad must have felt sorry for me because he bought me a nice rod and reel. Fink's Lake, Jones Lake, Nichols Lake and Lowe Lake surrounded Stockbridge, and a creek ran right through town.

I spent more time in the woods and at the lakes because it was safer. There was a gang of older boys in town who went out of their way to remind me that I was an Indian and unwelcome. If I went downtown, I walked there in the middle of the street to insure a few steps' advantage if they appeared. They caught me only twice. After that, I found escape routes over fences and through backyards that were a lot faster than the street routes these guys took.

Public school was something else altogether. It became a place of intimidation and preferential treatment. At times there was outright discrimination and no one to appeal to for protection because I did not know whom I could trust. All I wanted was to be accepted as an equal. That never happened. There were a few who were my friends, but I am always amazed at their ignorance of what I was going through at the time. After visiting with others of our people I found this was not uncommon. To most students and faculty I was an alien in their midst.

I remember one of the first history classes I was assigned to take, Early American History. By then, everyone knew I was an Indian—not that I could hide it. I look Indian. When the subject matter began recounting the pilgrims' and settlers' experiences with Indians, the terms "dirty heathen savages," "godless pagans" and "bloodthirsty Indians" were read aloud from the text. With the pronouncement of each word, almost as if on cue, every student in the room would turn and stare at me.

In the beginning, I believed what was written about us. I was ashamed and felt guilty and would lower my head and look at the floor. By the time the school year was over I hardly lifted my head at all. I didn't think I had any right to expect anything better than I was getting from my fellow students and the boys who hunted me.

Dad was exhibiting nearly all of the symptoms that have been linked to historical trauma—to the boarding schools and to lifelong prejudice that he had known. He, too, had inherited the struggles of the seven generations before him as what we call blood memory, which in Western culture is called genetic memory. He was an alcoholic, and it was hard to know the right time to approach him. He flew into rages at some of the smallest incidences.

His pain, it seemed, was so deep-seated that he did not know how to expel it, and I became his target. One moment, he was a loving dad taking me hunting, fishing or just playing around in the backyard. The next, he was knocking me around or forcing me to sit or stand by his chair for hours at a time. I was not to move or speak.

I remember eating meals with him glaring across the table with rage, gritting his teeth and breathing hard. I remember dreading his footsteps through the house. I remember him coming home from a period of hospitalization, hugging us all, and then taking me out to check on my yard work. I was so happy to have him come home, but he berated everything I did, calling me stupid and telling me how incompetent I was.

I was never allowed to hold his hand or sit in his lap. The only time he took an interest in what I was doing was when I was playing sports.

In one particularly violent episode, my dad was drunk and attacked my mother. I tried to step between them and defend her. I was 10. He picked up a baseball bat on the porch and started after me, yelling, "When I catch you I am going to kill you!"

I ran from the house through the garden and into a vacant lot at the end of our street. Dad was too drunk to chase me, but the only thing I was thinking about was getting away. When I realized he was no longer behind me, I started thinking about where I could go and whom I could tell. I did not feel I could go back to the house. But I also felt no one would believe me. Dad was not like this outside our home. He got drunk with his friends, but he was not violent around them. I remember feeling totally alone.

I was not a churchgoer and did not read the Bible, but in my outdoor experiences amid the beauty of Creation I had come to believe in a Higher Power. In the vacant lot, I lifted my hands toward the sky and cried, "God! Help me!"

Immediately, I felt a great surge of energy around me. I was not afraid; I was more in awe of what was happening to me. I cannot explain adequately all that took place, but I felt suspended from the earth. There were utterances coming out of me that I did not understand and I heard other utterances coming from somewhere outside me. I don't know how long this went on, but when I came to myself I was no longer afraid. I also felt a calling in my spirit that has remained to this day.

I went back to the house and peered in the windows to get Mom's attention and find out if "the coast was clear." She motioned me inside. Dad had fallen asleep.

There were things about Stockbridge that give me pleasure still. I had a few friends, and we remain friends today. I remember the wagonloads of wheat during the harvest being pulled into town day and night by tractors and loaded into boxcars. I also remember the smell that wafted through town as trucks came through with harvested peppermint on their way to the mint still at the edge of town that produced flavoring for peppermint gum and candy.

There was a fishing hole in the creek and in order to reach it, I had to cross Clare Riggs' pasture. His wife, Luella, worked at the Sweet Shop downtown. I usually would be with my dog, Skipper. He was my best friend, a cross between a collie and a German shepherd, and he ruled the other dogs around town. The gang of boys who chased me knew to avoid me if Skipper was with me. Skipper enjoyed going to the fishing hole almost as much as I did.

I don't know what prompted Clare Riggs to buy a Hereford bull, let alone a mean one, but he did. One day, I was halfway across the pasture on my way to the fishing hole when I noticed the bull was on his way to intercept me. This bull was huge. I started running for the fence, calling Skipper as I ran. I rolled under the fence seconds before the bull arrived.

Skipper got there at the same time and went after the bull. The bull chased him but Skipper was faster and ran in circles, ending up behind the bull. Skipper reached out and bit down on the bull's hamstring, pulling the bull down into the field. Every time we went by that pasture after that, Skipper would chase the bull and pull him down. Skipper would come back prancing and strutting at his conquest, wanting me to give him special attention for his deed.

One day, I walked into the Sweet Shop and did not see Clare Riggs come out from one of the aisles. He grabbed me by the front of my shirt, nearly lifting me off the floor, and ranted, "You ruined my bull." His wife, Luella, was behind the counter and ordered Clare to let me go, saying, "You got what you deserved. You should have never put that bull in that pasture anyway."

It was difficult to get ready for school each year because of the conditions I have already mentioned. In the 6th grade, I signed up for Safety Patrol and was assigned to a street corner. It was my responsibility to be at this post at certain times each day, before and after school. There was a new principal at the school and I did not like him.

One day, I was late getting to school from my patrol corner and, as I entered the building, the principal met me at the door. He grabbed me by my shirt and twisted it around my neck until I was choking. He tightened his grip—yelling at me until I nearly passed out—before letting go. To this day I can still see his twisted face and grinding teeth as he lifted me off the floor. The windows to the school offices made us visible, but no one came to my rescue that day.

I met a girl when I started junior high. She was a farm girl, and we became friends. I enjoyed going out to her father's farm on weekends and helping with chores, just to be around her. It was nice to have someone like her in my life at that point.

The farm was six miles from town. With permission I would leave on Saturday morning and cut across country on foot, returning home on Sunday afternoon.

I was 14 when, one Sunday, I walked into the house and felt tension. Dad looked up from his easy chair and said, "Why don't you pack your damn bags and move out there!" I started to respond, and he jumped up and knocked the wind out of me. He stood before me, yelling in my face. When I got my wind back—I don't know what came over me, but—I grabbed him and pushed him down into his chair, with my weight on top of him.

Dad had been a semipro lightweight fighter: no one doubted his ability to defend himself and I knew if I let him go, he would do some damage. He screamed obscenities as he tried to get me off of him. I told him he had hit me for the last time and that if he ever hit me again, I was going to fight him.

Mom tried to pull me off. Finally, I stood up and Dad went into this rage, stalking back and forth and telling me what he was going to do to me if I ever touched him again. Knowing his aggressive tendencies, Mom was so afraid the threat would come to pass that on Monday morning, she and my grandfather moved me out of the house to a distant farm.

The man who owned the farm was a friend of Grandpa's and a former police truant officer. I had a paper sack with my clothes. I was made to sit down in the farmer's front room, and he gave orders concerning my conduct and his expectations of me. I was then directed to my bedroom upstairs.

I had been banished. When I arrived at school and went to find my brother, he told me that Dad had instructed him and my two sisters to tell me that I was no longer their brother. I think I was numb. I really missed Skipper.

I got up every day at 4:30 a.m., put on my barn clothes and helped with the milking. Then I cleaned the barn, shoveled manure into a wheelbarrow and put down disinfectant in preparation for the afternoon milking. I then went back into the house, took a bath, put on my school clothes, ate breakfast and got on the bus.

I had been banished in late fall. The next spring, the farmer started building a new milk house next to the barn. He had a small tractor with a box on the back: I carried the milk pails from the barn, loaded them into the box and drove them down to the old milk house, where I dumped the milk into the cream separators.

The front block walls of the new milk house were near completion. One day, as I was backing up to the barn to load the next bunch of milk cans, I shut the tractor off, let the clutch out too quickly, and the tractor lurched backward and knocked down the new walls. My first instinct was to run, but I decided to go tell the farmer what had happened. He dropped his pitchfork and ran through the barn, and then all I could hear was ranting and raving. I was not going to face him when he came back—and had no idea where I would be banished to next—so I ran. I stuck to the woods and along ditches until I came out on a road, two miles away. I was trying to think of where I might go, but nothing came to mind.

So I turned, and started back to the farm to face the music. When I arrived at the farm, Dad's car was out front and my paper bag full of clothes was on the backseat. I got in and rode home.

We had a two-bedroom house and all six of us lived in it; my brother and I even shared a bed. You can only imagine the turbulence of feelings coursing through me as I reentered the house. Nothing was said by anyone, and I put my things where they had been before I was taken away. I still had Skipper, the woods and lakes and my dreams, but not much else.

I started thinking about the day when I could leave. I don't know what triggered it, but I prayed to the Creator that He would show me the woman I was to spend my life with. And He did. In a dream I saw a young woman walking down the street.

I was near finishing the ninth grade and the school year was almost over. I don't have much memory of any of it. Maybe when one goes through such terrible things, his memory is effected: Maybe I just don't want to remember. But Dad came home from work one day and he and Mom gathered us together to announce that we were moving to Lansing, the state capitol.

The thought of moving to a large city was overwhelming. My only sanctuary had been the outdoors, away from town: How in the world was I going to get there from a city like Lansing?

Dad rented a truck, and we moved. I wept all the way, dreading everything to come. The new, unfamiliar house; the polluted Grand River, which flowed through the city and was filled with carp and stink; and going to a new school, where I was treated as an outsider both because I had not attended any of the city's junior high schools and because I was the only student who was identified as Indian.

I certainly did not trust anyone, and did not go out of my way to make friends. To this day I have no contact with any student from Sexton High School, although that is probably more of my fault than anyone else's. I had no intention of creating new problems for myself, but I did so anyway.

I felt so threatened in my new environment that one morning, I went to my locker, put on my gym shoes and started walking to Stockbridge. I left at about 8:30 a.m. and arrived in Stockbridge eight hours later, covering a distance of more than 40 miles. I begged my grandpa to let me stay with him and finish school there.

I did not understand that Grandpa was too old—Grandma had passed away—to have the energy to deal with a teenage boy. He called my parents and they came and got me. On the way back, Dad said, "I can't stop you from running away, but the next time you do and we come and get you, I am putting you in a boy's training school." That was not a place I wanted to go, so I decided to endure the situation I was in.

I had discovered I could fight, and had developed a reputation. My nickname was "Renegade," and I liked it. In my junior year I remember a teacher describing an early American history class we were going to take, and he ended by saying, "We are going to study military geniuses like General George Armstrong Custer and the dirty heathen savages that killed him!"

There were gasps throughout the room, as every head turned to see what I was going to do. In other situations, I had made my taunters pay dearly, but this time I wanted to show my fellow students that I did have a tamer side. I raised my hand, was acknowledged by the teacher and told him, "I would appreciate it if you would not call my ancestors 'dirty heathen savages!'" and sat down. The teacher spent the rest of the school year apologizing.

I discovered art and writing in school. The two teachers that had the most influence on me were the art teacher, Mr. James Bonner, and the college-level English teacher, Mrs. Evelyn Cooke.

In 10th grade, I wrote a term paper and stated, "I have been born 250 years out of time. I do not belong here." Mrs. Cooke gave me a good mark for the paper and did her best to be a counselor to me, encouraging me and telling me that I had value and belonged. Mr. Bonner praised my art and wanted me to go into car design. Given all my negative experiences with other teachers and fellow students, these two teachers were bright lights in my darkness, and I will never forget them.

I did not obtain particularly good grades in high school, but I did graduate. I did not have a sports jacket or a pair of dress shoes for the ceremony, but my uncle sent me one of his jackets and I wore a pair of my dad's shoes. When I got home, I found five dollars in one of the jacket pockets; I called my uncle to tell him about the money, and he told me it was for me.

That fall, I went to work at General Motors Corp. It was the last job I wanted, but GM was the first employer that would hire me. I did not like working in a plant, doing mindlessly repetitive tasks every day to collect a paycheck. I had watched my father age this way and not care what happened to himself.

I wanted something better, and had a gnawing premonition that I needed to be somewhere else, doing something more satisfying than building cars. But I had started drinking heavily and was well on my way to being an alcoholic. I was also addicted to cigarettes and smoked two to three packs a day. My drinking had carried me into places and situations that, had I been caught, would have landed me in jail. But through all my carelessness and wantonness, the Creator kept me.

I married at 19 and was on my way to divorce two months later. I had forgotten the dream about the woman I was supposed to wait for and, in my drunken stupor, had gotten myself into a situation that would take two and a half years to free myself from. My wife cross-filed for divorce and left the state, but she continued to pay a lawyer who kept me in limbo.

Three years later, my grandpa passed away. Mom inherited his house and she, my dad, my siblings and I moved back to Stockbridge. One afternoon, I was headed downtown and saw this girl walking home from school. It was the girl I had seen in my dream seven years before. Two months later, we were married.

The vision I had seen of my life's journey was accelerating. This girl—Barbara—brought a quality to my life that only she could have. How could I have known I would come back to Stockbridge and meet her? How could she have known that her father would move his family from Illinois to Stockbridge, so that she could meet me? God has a way of ordering things, if we are patient enough to wait for them.

We are taught that life is a matrix of concentric circles. Mine seemed to be spiraling upward to a better place than I had known.

Dancing My Dream

There is a song dancing through my heart, reminding me of quieter times and more peaceful ways. I hear the voices of the ancestors singing, and I feel their reverence as they sing about these things.

I live in a world that is foreign to every fiber of my being, and I often try to drift away to join those ancestors in that memory. When it is time for me to wake up, I resist. "Let me live in this reverie just a while longer!" I plead. I want to remain there until the last note of their voices fades away.

It is my ancestors who want me to represent them to our children and those generations yet unborn. They want me to tell these generations who the ancestors were, and how they came to be known as Waganakising Odawa.

I will tell them about the Big Pine that signaled our fishermen to come ashore. I will speak of the Seven Grandfathers, and how the Creator gave us these gifts. I will share with them the sacredness of our lives and our connection to the Old Ones. I will encourage them to pray and to remember that they are more spirit than flesh and blood. I will speak of the Shimauganish, the warriors who fought the invaders, and of what they were willing to die for to try to preserve our sacred way of life.

I will sing the warrior songs, and I will sing of love and of reverence for life and all life-giving things. I will hold my children and grandchildren close to my heart and do all that

I can to help them avoid the pain and anguish that once troubled my soul.

I am the great-great-grandson of Ignatius Petoskey, whose Odawa name was Biidassige, which means "Early Morning Light" or "One Who Brings the Light." He was called Biidassige because of the time of day he was born, and because the Elders had seen a sign from the Creator of his impending birth: a sliver of light on the horizon right before the sun appeared. To me, the name Biidassige also foretold my great-great-grandfather's Life Path and the promise of a better day for our people. I believe there is an indelible genetic imprint on my life because of him.

In 1954, when I was 9, my Great Auntie Ella Jane Petoskey—Biidassige's granddaughter—asked me to carry his name. Asking such a thing is a custom among our people, and it is not entered into lightly. She also told me that my life would take a different path than that of most people. When I asked her what she meant by that, she mysteriously replied, "You will find out!"

It was with this consciousness that my dreams, visions and experiences have brought me to the place where I am today. I am "One Who Brings the Light."

But it was not until 1986 that I began to understand that Biidassige carries greater spiritual significance than mere personal recognition or a name called out in a traditional ceremony.

That year, as vice president of the Northern Michigan Ottawa Association*, I attended a Native American reaffirmation conference in Petoskey, a wealthy northern Michigan resort town named after my great-great-grandfather. It was held at the Perry-Davis Hotel, and at the first break I went for a walk; in a part of the building where I was alone, an old Indian man approached and asked me my name. When I said "Petoskey," he said, "I am going to tell you where your name came from," and went on to tell me the same story my Great Auntie had shared at the time of my naming. During the entire time he spoke to me I shook visibly, and in my mind

I heard a voice whispering over and over, "For some have entertained messengers unaware! For some have entertained messengers unaware!" My Great Auntie's prophesy about the direction my life would take was being reaffirmed by this old man, whom I had never seen before and never saw again.

I will just use the name Grandfather Biidassige when referring to my great-great-grandfather in this book. His father's name was Neias. Some people who do not understand our traditions might call Neias a Frenchman, but he was formally adopted into our tribe. He became an Odawa, married an Odawa woman and lived his life as a traditional Odawa, not as a Frenchman. In our long tradition—and this has been reaffirmed by our traditional spiritual guides and teachers of today—we are who our hearts say we are.

Grandfather Biidassige was born in 1797 in the northwest corner of what today is Michigan's Lower Peninsula. He and his family lived in a wigwam near Seven Mile Point, near what today is the tiny hamlet of Good Hart.

Catholicism had already established itself in our midst, and priests were busy trying to convince our people to join the church and abandon their traditional beliefs and practices. They sought permission from parents to send their children to Catholic schools. Grandfather Biidassige refused, and he became the focus of the priests' ridicule. He was ostracized by them.

My Grandfather Biidassige was a warrior. He was an acquaintance of the great Shawnee warrior Tecumseh, and he probably fought in the War of 1812 as part of the British-Indian military alliance to stop the American advance northward. He would have been 15.

Grandfather Biidassige tried to find a way to stay at Seven Mile Point, and to maintain his consciousness and loyalty to the teachings of his ancestors without being a threat to the mission. But that proved to be impossible, and in the quiet of night he loaded his family and belongings in *jiimaans* (canoes) and made his way east up the coast of Lake Michigan to a small Odawa village called Mukwa Zebing, on Little Traverse

Bay. Eventually, he and his sons established a trading post, as visitors began arriving from Chicago, having heard of the area's beauty and tranquility.

In 1836, Grandfather Biidassige and his sons bought 440 acres of land from the U.S. government to create a sanctuary for others living along the bay's northern shore who did not want to sign consent papers and allow the priests to send their children away. Grandfather Biidassige was 39 when he made his purchase. He was looking for a legal way for us to continue to live as we had in the old village, before the priests' arrival.

It was not to be. The following year Michigan became a state, and the federal government didn't bother to transfer the deed of ownership on the land to the new state government. Grandfather Biidassige was unaware that he had to pay state property taxes and, in due time, a Presbyterian minister showed up with a deed to 80 acres of his land, which he had purchased for back taxes. Grandfather Biidassige lost one-fifth of his sanctuary, and the pressure was on: He knew that contesting the sale might result in the transfer of all the Odawa living in the area to Kansas. Recognized as an *ogima* (headman) for his leadership ability, Grandfather Biidassige had to find a way for the North Shore families to survive.

Grandfather Biidassige's world was changing markedly. A city was rising out of the earth and surrounding his trading post, as a steady stream of foreigners continued to arrive daily to occupy the land that was once the homeland only of Odawa. He had to develop the skills to live in one world—a world not of his choosing—while keeping his feet and heart centered in another in order to maintain his sanity. It is no different for us today.

---

*The Odawa (Oh-DAH-wuh) and the Ottawa are the same people. The Europeans heard the original pronunciation as "Ottawa."

Affirmation

My earliest memories of Waganakising are of visiting my Great Auntie Ella Jane Petoskey's home near Seven Mile Point.

Waganakising is the place where our summer grounds were located. In the Odawak language the word means "it is bent," and refers to a great white pine that grew on the shore near Good Heart, which is now Good Hart. Great Auntie lived in a small cabin in the middle of the woods, west of Harbor Springs.

My visits to see her were mystical and ethereal in so many ways. Great Auntie entered the world in 1880 and walked on in 1972, at age 92, so she witnessed the dramatic transformation of our people. She was a survivor of the Carlisle Indian Industrial School in Carlisle, Pennsylvania, one of the first and most notorious of the Indian boarding schools.

I heard Great Auntie speak in the beautiful, poetic language of our grandfathers—*Anishinaabemowin,* the original language of the Great Lakes region—knowing that it once was the only language spoken here. The rocks, trees, waters and Mother Earth knew this language. At the age of 6, on one of my visits, I remember taking my shoes off to feel this place with the soles of my bare feet. The sensations rose up my legs, filled my heart and touched my soul.

I knew even then, though I did not live among our people, that I was *Waganakising* Odawa. That knowledge fueled my long search for my true home and family and a greater understanding of my identity. The dreams I experienced spoke to me of a good life and of a time when there was peace and sanctuary for us as a people; a way of life that I still long for.

I heard Great Auntie speak of our Odawak village, which extended from near Bay Shore, on the south side of Little Traverse Bay, all the way to Good Hart. She described children at play and the adult activities that permeated the village each day. It was not hard for my child's imagination to envision that long-vanished place. Perhaps the reason I could "see" it was because of my ancestry—or maybe it was just because I wanted to know it so badly.

Great Auntie told me how Odawak women hummed as they prepared meals, thinking good thoughts over the food so their families would think good thoughts as they ate it. She told of young girls being taught by their mothers, aunties and grandmothers, knowing that one day they, too, would be mothers, aunties and grandmothers; and of young men being taught by their fathers, uncles and grandfathers, knowing that one day they would fill those positions.

In the old ways, there were no greater offices than those of Clan Mother and Elder. Traditional people still hold and treasure those positions today.

Great Auntie told me that a squirrel could climb a tree at Good Hart and never touch the ground until it reached the banks of Lake Huron, on the opposite side of (what today is) the state of Michigan. She said the canopy from the giant trees prevented sunlight from reaching the earth. She said there were clear pathways through the forest because of this, but that is no longer. In the 19th and 20th centuries, the lumber industry destroyed all but a few remnants of the state's virgin forests.

We knew that the great bounty we enjoyed did not belong to us. We believed the Creator had placed us here to be caretakers of His garden. That garden was our tabernacle, where we worshipped and revered our lives.

It was considered dishonorable to even consider trying to dominate the environment. We saw ourselves as mere strands in the Creator's great weaving of life-giving things. We hunted, fished, gathered and gardened. We gave thanks every day for these gifts. We always gave thanks.

We knew that the things the Creator had spoken into existence were all part of a web, and that each strand was dependent on every other strand. We called the rocks "grandfathers," believing they spoke to us of Mother Earth's unfathomably long history and of our own relationship to Her. We did not view rocks as inanimate objects, but counted them among the many life-giving things the Creator had spoken into existence. Many of us still believe these things, though sadly, we are too few.

Grandmother Sun and Grandmother Moon were our teachers. We knew we were only a part of the vast universe: not greater or lesser, just a part. So it was a part of our consciousness to recognize and honor the interconnectedness of all living things. We breathed in fresh air, knowing that the plants and trees needed the carbon dioxide we exhaled as surely as we needed the oxygen they returned.

While we, the *Anishinaabeg**, were the caretakers of Turtle Island, human beings could drink from any stream and consume fish and venison without fear of contamination. The environment around us was not considered a "wilderness," and it only became so with the arrival of the European *Waisichu* (a Lakotah word that means "fat-takers").

There was no sickness or disease among us, and our people lived well beyond 100 years. When the *Waisichu* came, they brought their diseases with them and we began to die. It was good that they wanted to be free, but they brought the habits of their grandfathers with them.

There was no fear or danger before the arrival of the Europeans. Our lives were peaceful. The sound of laughter rang from our villages, heralding our consciousness. We loved this life the Creator had designed for us. We arose at sunrise and met the sunset of each day with thanksgiving for the wonderful things the Creator had supplied.

This great light that climbed into the sky each day and the softer light that introduced each evening reminded us of the Creator's love for us. When darkness fell and another day ended, people went to their dwellings to be lulled to sleep by the crickets and the whippoorwills. We arose the next day in the early morning light with the songs of the morning birds as our alarm clock.

It was so quiet at times that one could hear a mouse playing in the leaves. Elders would sit for long periods of time and never speak. Quiet was an important time: Quiet was relished and appreciated. No one was in a hurry. To hurry was to make mistakes and miss things of importance.

Courtesy, love, honor and respect were the order of every day.

When a woman was giving birth, our custom was to gather outside the dwelling and, when we heard the first sounds of new life, we would look for a sign to name the newborn; we believed the Creator attended the birth. It was exciting because it was understood that the Creator would provide a name that would be part of that child's identity for his or her life and later. It was an understanding that he or she was a gift and would always be recognized as a sacred being. We knew that life did not come forth because a man and woman coupled, but because the Creator alone determines life. Through the naming ceremony, we also reminded one another of our sacred origins and of our eventual sacred reunion with our ancestors.

In late fall, hunters began preparations for their journey to the hunting grounds, which were located in what today is Wisconsin and Minnesota. Tools were made ready, including stone knives, hatchets, bows and arrows. If the hunters failed in their mission it would be a long, cold and hungry winter for the tribe.

Young men accompanied the hunters to learn how to hunt and to care for the meat and hides. They made their way through the islands, now called Beaver Island, High Island and Garden Island, to Martin's Island and on across Lake Michigan to what is now the Door Peninsula of eastern Wisconsin and separates Green Bay from Lake Michigan.

At the hunting grounds there were buffalo, deer, caribou and moose. When sufficient meat had been harvested, the men loaded the *jiimaans* and traveled to the winter grounds, southwest of what today is Chicago between Effingham and the Mississippi River. Their families—the Elders, women and children of *Waganakising*—would arrive at the winter grounds about a month earlier, to prepare for the arrival of the hunters.

Some of the trip was by trail but most of it was by water, down rivers and across lakes. There were no clocks and there was no problem finding a place to camp for the night because there were no "No Trespassing" signs. Men from different tribes met and agreed there would be no trouble. The success of the hunt was too important to all of them.

At the winter grounds, longhouses left from past winters were repaired and covered with bark from the slippery elm, to ward off the rain and provide insulation from the cold. Everyone eagerly anticipated the hunters' arrival and the feast they all would enjoy.

Winter was a time for storytelling. It also was the time to make new clothing and moccasins. There was feasting and happiness. The longhouses allowed many families to live together; during the day, the women visited and the children played.

Spring announced the time to begin the northward journey back to Waganakising.

It was a good journey, because we stopped to visit our brothers and sisters in other tribal encampments along the way.

It was on one such return trip in 1797 that Grandfather Biidassige was born at the mouth of the Manistee River at first light.

I loved visiting Great Auntie in her cabin in the middle of the woods. She touched my life in a way no else could. I could see the ancestors and the life we once had through her eyes and her stories.

I live today in this altered state, knowing there was a time when the Waganakising Odawa were the only people inhabiting this place. I have no desire to be anything but Indian. When my time comes to walk on, I know my spirit will return to its origin. It is my wish that my bones will rest here at *Waganakising* with the bones of my ancestors, and that the Circle of Life will once more be revisited.

Anishinaabe (singular) and *Anishinaabeg* (plural) refer to the three main tribes of Great Lakes Indians: the Odawa, the Ojibwa and the Potawatomi.

Negation

It was obvious to me that Great Auntie loved my father. Her visits to our home were more spiritual in nature than social.

Dad was long removed from his culture—angry, frustrated and in pain—and he was medicating himself with alcohol. He had been stripped of his language, his land, his cultural origins and a loving relationship with his own father because of the boarding school syndrome. He was haunted by the feeling of having been "exiled" from a life that should have been his—and all of ours.

As a boy, I knew none of this. It was much later that I discovered that both my grandfather and his sister, Great Auntie, had attended and graduated from Carlisle Indian Industrial School in Carlisle, Pennsylvania.

My grandfather came away from Carlisle not knowing how to be a father or a husband. He had been raised by the staff of the boarding school and had not been taught our traditional ways or experienced a traditional upbringing. He and my father did not get along. Dad had worked and saved money for college and his father had taken it. Dad would not talk about his father at all: if the subject was broached, he reacted with anger.

I also discovered that my father's older brothers and sisters had attended Mt. Pleasant Indian School, a government boarding school in Mt. Pleasant, Michigan.

My father said that the only reason that he, his brother Wayne and his youngest sister, Elaine, weren't taken was a lack of bed space. But he may not have wanted me to know the truth. I have a picture of him on the grounds of Mt. Pleasant with a group of young friends. Whether my father attended or not, he exhibited all of the dysfunctions mirrored in other boarding school survivors.

(Today, there is a display on the school at the *Ziibiwing* Center of *Anishinabe* Culture & Lifeways in Mt. Pleasant.)

The experience of being separated from his family was so traumatic that another of my father's brothers, Alvius, and a friend named Elmer Minor ran away from Mt. Pleasant: they jumped a passing freight train to try to escape. It was the middle of winter, and by the time the train reached its destination—Traverse City in northern Michigan—my uncle and his friend had nearly frozen to death. They were hospitalized and sent back to Mt. Pleasant.

Both men returned home damaged. Uncle Al would later spend two years in prison for robbery, although he was able to enter the service after his incarceration and distinguished himself as a member of the 1st Cavalry at the Battle of the Bulge in World War II. He retired from the military as a top sergeant.

The schools were "designed" to erase all consciousness of Indian language and culture and to "Americanize" their residents. The method used to insure this "training" was a strict military-style regimen. (What happened in the boarding schools had a far-reaching impact: In Germany in the mid-1930s, Nazi leaders who were studying racial purity became interested in—and published articles about—American policies toward Indians.)

Children as young as 6 were removed from their homes and sent to the schools for as long as six or seven years; many stayed through high school. Boys and girls had their hair cut and their clothes confiscated and were issued uniforms. Before they could put on the uniforms, they were made to bathe, were deloused with DDT and examined by a medical practitioner. A matron went down the line and extracted any discolored teeth without benefit of an anesthetic.

Many of the young girls underwent sterilization with no explanation of what the procedure meant or how it would change their lives.

Siblings were separated, and children saw their parents only rarely, if at all. They were forbidden to speak their language or practice their traditions, and each infraction was met with a graduating level of punishments, which included beatings. Some children whose ears were boxed developed hearing problems.

In the case of Carlisle, a student who continued to defy the rules was locked in an unheated, windowless building for three days without food or water. Many of these children died. In fact, one of the first students to return from Carlisle reported to his people that more children died at the school than made it home.

Some of the older children were defiant and gathered secretly to speak to each other, to keep their language and identities alive. It was natural for the younger children to develop emotional attachments to staff members and matrons, and in many cases, the attachments led to physical and sexual abuse.

The boarding schools created what psychologists call "intergenerational trauma." My grandfather, his sister and every generation of the Biidassige family since has been affected. Every family has been dysfunctional to a greater or lesser degree.

We have had family members do prison time and lose children to the state because of alcoholism; others joined religious cults in an attempt to "blend" into mainstream culture. Still others are mentally challenged, abandoned their families altogether or were murdered, and a certain level of family estrangement exists, which I now attribute to boarding school syndrome.

I can in no way address all of the syndrome's effects. My story is only one of thousands. There is much more that could be said and I know there are others who have their own stories to tell.

Most of the survivors of the Indian boarding schools took their stories to their graves. Most of those still alive—the majority of whom are in their 70s or older—still are unable to talk about their experiences. But some have started to share what has been repressed with other survivors, therapists, their families and, sometimes, even the public. Healing is just beginning. We have a long, long way to go.

Note: In 2006, the Canadian federal government—which for decades funded a system of Indian boarding schools similar to those in the United States—agreed to a reparation package for survivors. The token awards were made available in 2007—too late for most survivors, who already had died. But they were one of the first attempts to acknowledge and address the wholesale abuse of indigenous people in an established democracy. No similar reparations are expected to be made to the last survivors of the U.S. schools.

My People

I love my people.

No other people laugh like them or weep like them.

No other people sing and dance like they do.

No other people I know rise in the morning and give thanks to the Creator for another beautiful gift of day, and then thank the Creator again when the sun falls below the horizon for all that the day has brought.

No other people I know will greet you and welcome you like they do, and you know they are sincerely glad to see you and be in your presence.

No other people I know hold life itself to be so sacred that even the flowers and trees acknowledge their presence.

No other people I know will greet a stranger and offer shelter and a meal.

No other people I know will accept you just like you are, without judgment or expectations.

No other people I know will sit and listen to your story, considering it equal to their own.

No other people I know will talk about seeing the *Meghiizi* (eagle) and stopping to give thanks and leave their offering.

No other people I know will ask nothing more than to sit with you in silence, and you will feel honored to be in their presence.

No other people I know are greater caregivers and lovers of men's souls. They will hold you above themselves and honor you in a way that you have never been honored before. They will give you what they have and give these things in a way that will allow you to feel that you are not obligated to them in any way.

No other people I know will talk to you in reverent tones about their mothers and fathers, grandmothers and grandfathers, and as you listen, you will think that you even knew them, too.

No other people I know are more beautiful in countenance or more sacred in manner.

No other people I know honor life and all life-giving things in the manner these people do.

No other people I know will dance and sing long into the night, laughing as much when the last song is sung as they were when the first one was sung.

No other people I know see the sunrise and sunset in the same way these people do, or seek places where they can hear the mouse playing in the leaves. They will teach you lessons in life without your knowing that they have passed their knowledge on to you, borne on the winds of tradition; you are not only hearing them, but their ancestors and teachers as well.

No other people I know understand the interconnectedness of all things and are more reverent about life.

No other people I know do not assign any experience as being bad or good, but see all of these things as teachers and each of us as students learning about life.

No other people I know will express their belief in spiritual origin and understand spiritual destination like these people.

So when you look at their red faces, I hope you can see these things, and when these people speak, I hope you will hear what they are saying. I don't know of any other people like these people, for they are my people —my relatives—and I am grateful every day for the sacred moments I spend in their presence.

Entering the Circle

In 1969, I grew tired of the chaos, dependency and ill health I had introduced into my life through addictions to alcohol and nicotine.

I attended a church service and was baptized. I also had a great spiritual awakening and left with no appetite for either drinking or smoking. That awakening was just the beginning.

At the time we were living in Dansville, near Lansing. There were plenty of churches in the area, but I was not drawn to any of them. They were no different from several churches I had tried to attend when I was young—following my experience in the vacant lot—where I felt only cold shoulders and no sense of shared spirit.

The Apostolic Church was different. It was in Pontiac—a long drive from Dansville—but we often visited my wife's grandparents there (and they were church members), so one Sunday we all attended.

I believe the people in that church were sent by the Creator. They did not see my color. My wife and our daughter, Diana Lynn, were welcomed with open arms and expressions of love.

The night I was baptized, I felt I needed to go up to the minister. Was I being led? I thought so and still think so.

He asked me what he could do for me, and I blurted out that I needed to be baptized. I didn't know anything about baptism, but at that moment, it seemed essential. He agreed, and I was baptized by immersion in water while the name of

Jesus Christ was called over me. To me this was particularly significant, because when Indians were first introduced to Christianity, we could not accept the idea of a Holy Trinity. We knew only the Creator as the Great Creator. I have since come to believe that Jesus Christ is the Creator, enrobed in flesh and come to save us all.

In 1971, we moved to Pontiac to be closer to the church, and the people there continue to be among our closest friends. But I also came to realize that it was not enough just to be Indian. To be truly Indian was to be spiritual, and to be spiritual, I had to find a deeper meaning in my life.

Slowly, now that I was sober and healthier, the consciousness I had lived as a boy returned; everywhere I went I saw the Creator. Maybe it was not so much that I *saw* the Creator but that I *sensed* Him, as my consciousness shifted from what was artificial in my environment to what was original and part of His creation.

The passing of each season held awe in its promise. I wanted to live in each moment, knowing that it was going to arrive and then leave. I enjoyed living off the land as much as I could by hunting, fishing and gathering berries, mushrooms and other wild foods. Some did not understand this preoccupation, but I derived a greater sense of being a provider for my wife and children—by now we had four daughters—doing these things than by working as a shipping-and-receiving clerk at a state-run boys' training school.

I knew there was so much more to being Indian than just touching the earth with my bare feet at Great Auntie's cabin. I wanted to learn, but I was unsure of the questions I needed to ask—even unsure of how to approach those who may have had some answers. I will always honor those who befriended me, inviting me into their confidence and teaching me that I needed to bring *semma* (Indian-grown sacred tobacco) when I came to ask. If they could answer my question, they accepted the *semma*. If they couldn't, they would direct me to someone who could.

I did not care for cities with large populations: I was out of my element in such places, and still am to this day. One of my dreams was to be able to live in a place that was sparsely populated, where there were no fences. I wanted to raise our children in such a place and I wanted to help our people.

So, in 1978, Barb and I decided to move to the Keweenaw Bay, in Michigan's remote Upper Peninsula, 500 miles northwest of Pontiac. Of course, my first priority was to find a job, and the main employer was the Keweenaw Bay Indian Community.

I was hired to be an assistant to the education director for the Keweenaw Bay Band of Lake Superior Chippewa Indians. It was a heady position for someone like me. To go to work every day and see nothing but brown faces was intoxicating, and I was beginning to fulfill my dream of finding my people.

Despite being Odawa and Lakotah, I was accepted by the Chippewa; to be among them was exhilarating. For the first time, I was living in a place where it was acceptable to be Indian! I would receive far more from this community than I could ever hope to give.

That first year, it came as a great honor to be asked to be part of the planning committee for the first powwow in Keweenaw Bay in 100 years; federal laws had declared our way of worship criminal and had deprived us of our constitutional right to religious freedom for the past century. But the U.S. Congress had just passed the American Indian Religious Freedom Act and, at last, we were allowed to hold our powwows and practice our traditional way of worship openly.

It was a great time of joy and hope for all of us.

The *Jiingtamok* (the Gathering of the People Powwow) took place in July of 1978 and hundreds of Indians participated, many of them from the Great Lakes region. Some also came from Ontario and other parts of the United States.

In 1979—for the next powwow—I prepared regalia that was simple in design. I had no eagle feathers and was really apprehensive; I had danced before in civilian clothing, but because I had no regalia, had not participated in a Grand Entry.

As I prepared to enter the dance circle in the Grand Entry, I was asked to carry the Keweenaw Bay Chippewa Eagle Staff. This was an honor reserved for a tribal member who was a U.S. veteran, but the veterans wanted to honor me! I remember tears flowing as I danced the staff into the circle.

The Grand Entry announces the beginning of a *Jiingtamok* and is repeated before the evening dance session begins. Flags and eagle staffs carried by *Shimauganish* (veteran warriors)lead the procession of female and male dancers, which includes jingle dress dancers, grass dancers and fancy dancers. But the most beautiful part of the powwow is the entry of the young people, all dressed in their handmade regalia—dresses, pants and shirts—some made of deerskins, others of brightly colored cloth and all elaborately decorated with feathers, embroidery and beadwork of every color. I have heard non-Indian visitors express awe and emotion upon seeing this display.

I was taught that when I entered the circle in the Grand Entry, I was to honor the Creator and Life by inviting and representing all of my ancestors who had walked on. I always felt a sense of sacredness, like I was dancing my prayers.

I knew my simple dance regalia had been accepted, but later I felt a need to create a more traditional one. I was told to ask the Creator about this new regalia and how it should look, and I had a dream in which I saw myself dressed in a certain way.

I am Bear Clan, and Bear Clan colors are purple and black: those were the colors in my dream. I also saw myself in a medicine hat with eagle feathers in the back.

I had never constructed a bustle, which seemed too complicated for me to make. So I started the project slowly, and the results were acceptable. When I had been coordinator of an Indian education program downstate, I had made a pair of moccasins in a project with some young people, and they also became part of my regalia. Over the years, I had saved other project articles just because they looked good, and they became part of my growing regalia, too.

But one piece was truly special: a *concho*, or decorative piece, made from an antique Spanish silver coin. It was a gift from my dad, and had been taken off a Spanish *conquistador* who had wandered too far north. My dad presented it to me after I told him I was making my own regalia. He told me it had been passed down from father to son, through the generations in our family, and he wanted me to put it on my regalia, saying, "I will always dance with you." I pinned it on my medicine hat, where it was partially hidden by white feathers. I believed it was valuable to keep it hidden there.

The healing of my relationship with my dad had begun. We had much more work to do, but given all my father and I had gone through when I was young, you can imagine how I felt when I entered the *Jiingtamok* in that first Grand Entry. I felt pride, gratitude and a new wholeness.

My knowledge of who I am continued to grow among the Chippewa.

While I enjoyed my journeys into the wilderness areas reachable from my little world, I was not fully conscious of my connection with Mother Earth.

If I had been raised among my people, I would have known from my earliest memories and through my growth into adulthood what it meant to "honor life and all life-giving things." I would have understood that you do not harvest more than you need.

I did learn at an early age that when an Elder entered the room, you offered him or her your seat. One was to remain quiet unless spoken to, and encouraged to listen to what the Elder had to say. We were also taught to offer the Elder food or water upon his or her arrival, but I had never connected these practices with being an Indian.

Among the Chippewa I learned that we should not cut down trees or dig deep holes in Mother Earth, and my prayers took on greater meaning and direction. I became even more conscious of the Creator and of His Creation. I learned that every human being has a right to his or her story and to the telling of it; every story is to be considered as sacred as my own, which is what makes Indians such good listeners in an age when, it seems, listening has become a lost art.

I learned about the Medicine Wheel and the Seven Grandfather teachings of the *Anishinaabeg* peoples: wisdom, love, respect, bravery, honesty, humility and truth. Essentially, I learned how to walk among my own people and how to treat those who were not of our nation.

Great Auntie's prophecy of "You will find out!" continues to expand.

Sunset One

The sun is in the western sky as I ponder my journey to this place in my life.

I sit on the sand of this Great Lake, among the Grandfathers who hold the sand in place, with the memory that this is where many of my ancestors sat generations before me in moments like this.

I feel gifted and honored by the Creator for allowing me to be in this place at this moment in time; this beautiful land where the spirits of my ancestors are carried back and forth on the soft wind, dancing in the beauty of this moment, touching me to the core of my being.

I think, "There has never been a sunset like this one!" Then, looking to the east, I think, "Grandmother Moon is smiling at me in a special way this night, and the Creator has allowed me enough vision to see with eyes that come from my heart."

I say to myself "I will not pass this way again," so I will drink it all in like a thirsty man, in gratitude.

It is *Kchitwaa* (sacred). I was drawn here at this moment in my life. My spirit is calmed and my heart softened, withdrawing for these few moments from the struggle of my survival. I hear the rustling in the woods behind me as the night creatures stir, and in my other ear, the soft sounds of the endless waves of water reaching out to shore. I think I hear a great drum and singers, the sounds coming to me out of the distant darkness. I think of my loved ones, of all my relatives, of my ancestors who have walked on, and of my *Anishinaabeg* nation. This is *Kchitwaa*! *Kchitwaa*! Always *Kchitwaa*!

It is time to give thanks, knowing that this moment and the vision and understanding it is offering will be like no other on this journey of life.

Kchitwaa Creator!

Sunset Two

T he sun is in the western sky as I ponder my place in this life.

I am not as troubled as I once was, but sometimes I would like for Grandfather Biidassige to carry me away for a while, so that I could experience those moments my ancestors knew before our present trouble.

Carry me to the time when the only noises in the day were the wind and the song of the doves, sitting in the noon sun and honoring the Creator for their gift. Carry me to the time when nights were filled with the sounds of crickets and whippoorwills, singing as they always had.

I listen now from where I sit and wonder what happened to all these beautiful things. I know where they have gone, and for a moment, I am angry with the perpetrators. But then I realize there is One who created an order to everything under His sun, and that He knows better than I what to do. So I sit and dream. I think I can hear a drum in the distance, calling The People together again: That one more time before the end of all things on Earth, we can celebrate who we are and see one another not as segregated on reservations, but as all related, as belonging to one another.

I see so many of our young people struggling today, and am concerned because they see no hope or promise for their lives. Sometimes I think it would be easier to leave this world and join the ancestors, but then I am reminded that I have been brought to this time and place to help my people remember the time before the arrival of the Europeans, when life for us was beautiful and sacred.

We need to sing those songs again and honor those who left us the consciousness of that life. We need to honor their efforts to preserve our practices, ways and beliefs. I know that we cannot live in the past, and that we are only on a journey from our spiritual origin to our special destination. But it is the past that has helped form the present. I pray that the enemies of all mankind—colonialism and unchecked capitalism—are not successful in destroying our dream. I believe they will not be so long as we are determined to return to what we know to be true and to help those among us who are weak and frail. I believe that is why we are here.

This is *Kchitwaa*! *Kchitwaa*! Always *Kchitwaa*! *Kchitwaa* Creator!

Morning Prayer
of an Odawa

C reator:
You are clothed with honor and majesty.
You cover Yourself with light as a garment
and stretch out the heavens like a curtain.
You lay the leaves of Your chambers in the waters
and make clouds Your chariot.
You walk upon the wings of the wind.
You make Your angels' spirits
and Your messengers a flaming fire.
You laid the foundation of the Earth
and it should not be moved forever.
You covered it with the deep as with a cloak,
and the waters stood above the mountain.
At Your command they fled; at the sound
of Your thunder they hurried away.
You send the springs into the valleys,
running among the hills.
You water the hills from Your chambers.
Mother Earth is satisfied with the fruit of Your works.
You cause the grass to grow for the buffalo
and the herbs for our medicines

that man may bring food out of the Earth.
You appoint the moon for seasons
and the sun his rising and going down.
You look at the Earth and it trembles
in anticipation of Your touch.
You touch the hills and they smoke.
I will seek the way You choose for me,
for in that way is life and the way of honor
and respect, *Chi-Miigwech*!*
Creator! *Chi-Miigwech*!

---

* *Chi-Miigwech* means "many thanks."

Fishing

W e were poor when we first moved into the apartment in Stockbridge. Dad and Mom were paying $25 a month for a lower apartment in a house that belonged to Mom's step-grandfather. We lived across the street from the coal yards, but just beyond those was country. Country was the place I gravitated to at every opportunity.

I think Dad liked to fish as much as I did. In the spring of the year, after the snow melted and the waters in the creeks returned to normal, we traveled around to some of the streams that fed into a lake. Fish came upstream to spawn, and it was a good time to harvest a few for a meal.

My brother and I started out watching Dad fish, but it wasn't long before we had short cane poles; when we didn't, we made fishing poles from straight sticks and tied our lines to the sticks. I liked fishing because I liked to eat fish, and because fish didn't cost anything outside of the expense for hooks, sinkers and bobbers. Once Dad was satisfied that we could graduate to better equipment, he bought Jon and me fishing poles with reels. From this point on, I was not satisfied to fish the small creeks around town. Fink's Lake was two miles outside town, Nichols Lake was a mile away, Jones Lake was two miles away and Lowe Lake was five miles away. The fishing possibilities these lakes offered drew me to walk to whichever lake was of interest at the time.

We had a chicken coop where Grandpa kept his laying hens, and the chicken yard was a prime place for finding worms and night crawlers. I had a little artificial bait, but worms and night crawlers were my baits of choice. I would slip out of the bedroom window between four and five o'clock in the morning to walk to one of these lakes and spend the entire day. When the sun was high in the sky and it was hot, I went swimming. It was important to be careful because nearly every one of these lakes had an unstable shoreline made up of muck or marl. People had drowned in some of them.

It was not the pursuit of a prize that motivated me to fish; it was the thought of having a fish dinner and helping with food costs. I asked my 81-year-old mother recently how many dinners I provided with the fish I brought home. She told me that it was quite a few.

I have never considered myself a sport fisherman or sport hunter. Looking back, what I was doing was similar to what my ancestors had done for hundreds of years. I don't believe in taking a fish for sport. The fish dinners were better than the boiled beef tongue or beef heart my mother would negotiate for at the local meat market (in those days, these parts of the cow were thrown away).

Looking back, it seems that the influence of my ancestors somehow had become a part of my consciousness. I did not know of anyone around me who thought this way, and it made me feel even more out of place.

To be successful as a fisherman was more than putting a worm on a hook and throwing it into a lake. There were places where the fish were prevalent and there were other places where they weren't. I was not going to walk some of the distances I did and spend the day, only to come home empty-handed.

I enjoyed ice fishing more than summer fishing. Grandpa had an ice shack with a kerosene heater in it. The hole we fished in was a foot and a half wide and two feet long. It was like looking into a fish aquarium: I watched fish appear in the depths below the hole and learned how to tease them into biting, even when it appeared they were going to ignore the bait suspended in the water.

One of my first trips ice fishing was with my grandfather. Grandpa owned a 1928 Model "A" Ford. We were going to South Lake, where Grandpa had put his ice shack for that winter's fishing. Grandpa pulled down to the ice, and started driving onto the lake with his car; I stopped him and asked to get out and walk. I did not think the ice would hold the car up, and did not want to be in the car if it went through. Grandpa understood and let me out, chuckling under his breath.

Dad had an ice shack on Lowe Lake, but he never drove his vehicle on the lake. During one of our trips there, Dad, my brother and I were sitting in the shanty and looking down into the hole when a muskrat popped onto the shanty floor from under the ice. The muskrat realized right away that he was not alone and started trying to bite in every direction. We were all dancing around, trying to avoid the muskrat's teeth and hollering at one another. Dad was laughing as the muskrat jumped back into the hole; we had danced well enough that no one had been bitten. My brother asked Dad later what would have happened if he had fallen into the hole. Dad said he would have had to spear him in his hinder parts. My brother and I didn't like the picture Dad had painted, and kept our distance from the hole in the ice.

Years later, I could not imagine allowing my son to do what I had done as a boy. It is a different and far more dangerous world than the one in which I grew up. The opportunity to fish and be around the lakes was like a tonic, and I hold fond memories of my experiences.

I still fish, but in very different waters.

When I was young, my grandpa subscribed to Field & Stream and Outdoor Life magazines. When he was through with them he would pass them on to me. I read countless articles on fishing for different types of fish and was always intrigued with Great Lakes fishing—especially with fishing in the coldest and deepest of the lakes, Superior.

In 1978, when we moved to Keweenaw Bay—the largest bay in the western Upper Peninsula—we lived on one of its inlets, Huron Bay. I was looking for work, but living on a bay and knowing it was connected to the Great Lake of Superior was a childhood dream come true. I caught trout from the dock, but I was most looking forward to ice fishing.

I knew little about fishing in these kinds of waters, but I had a few friends in the area who were willing to take me under their wing and teach me, and I learned quickly. I always believed that fresh fish and game were better in one's diet than the processed foods in stores. So it was important to me to be somewhat proficient at harvesting both to help feed our growing family. Our kids enjoyed fish, partridge, rabbit and venison.

That first winter, one of my good friends invited me to go with him to catch whitefish. At that time whitefish were plentiful because no one was harvesting them—except for an occasional fish caught by accident. Whitefish are not easy to catch because they have soft mouths and because of the manner in which they feed.

We were sitting in an ice shack when a large school of smelt minnows came through the hole. All of a sudden they scattered, and we could see larger fish among them, slapping the minnows with their tails and butting them with their heads. The stunned minnows sank in their struggle to gain their balance in the water. The whitefish sucked them up along the bottom.

Another day, my friend and I fished on the other side of Huron Bay, off a place called Pine Point. We chopped holes in the ice with our spud. I was using the butt section of my spinning rod and a Swedish pimple as a lure. I remembered what I had seen in the shanty, with the whitefish stunning the smelt minnows and then feeding on the ones that sank to the bottom. I dropped my lure to the bottom of the lake, about 40 feet down, and started bouncing it around to try to make it look as much like a stunned smelt as I could.

That afternoon I caught seven whitefish, and from that day on, whitefish would become the object of my fishing. Over the next several years, I averaged catching 300 pounds of whitefish each winter through the ice.

It was not easy. I often walked up to six miles on the ice, punching holes that ranged from a foot thick to three feet thick and searching for the schools of whitefish that I knew inhabited the bay. It was important to put *semma* down and give thanks for the fish that would help us. In those days I was able to endure cold temperatures a lot better than I am now, and I often fished in temperatures below zero, sitting on the ice without a shelter. I never thought of it as a hardship. If I got too cold I had only to get up and move and punch another hole in the ice—and by the time I was ready to fish, I was warm again.

The quality of the area's whitefish fishing reached other fishermen and, eventually, it was not uncommon to have a "city" on the ice. Initially there were two women who had been catching whitefish on a regular basis for years, and they had done a good job keeping it quiet. I have never been one to reveal my fishing secrets, either, but some of those who fished for lake trout got curious about our activity. Those of us who fished for whitefish all knew one another; we were either neighbors or had met at the local coffee shop. There was a lot of camaraderie and bantering back and forth, but many of those guys have walked on.

A while back, I went into the local sporting goods store, only to find several men talking about the days when whitefish fishing was good and sharing some of the humorous incidents that had taken place.

I said that, as unbelievable as it might seem, I used to walk out onto the bay at a place called the "A-Frame" and start punching holes, trying to find whitefish, and work my way all the way down to the rock dock two miles away. Then I'd cross the bay and punch holes on the other side, searching for whitefish.

One man, Smitty, spoke up and said that anyone who questioned my account should be directed to him. He said that many of the fishermen out there watched me.

Smitty went on to tell a story that I did not know about: A friend of his was fishing near him, and decided to move some distance away and try a new spot. Smitty said that I came along and dropped my line in the hole this guy had just abandoned and, over the next hour, caught my limit of whitefish—12—and went home. He said his buddy came back over after watching this and vowed to get up early the next morning and beat me back to the spot. Smitty said that the next day, I walked out on the ice. His buddy was fishing in the hole and offered to give it to me if I wanted it. I told him I would rather go and fish in the second hole the guy had made the day before. Smitty said that again, I caught my limit and that his buddy was seething. I don't remember the incident.

Whitefish are still being caught, but not in the numbers they were in those days, because of the increase in commercial fishing. As an Indian, it was and is important to me to remember to offer prayers of thanksgiving anytime I harvest fish or game; these creatures belong to the Creator as much as I do.

To fish and hunt helped me stay conscious of the old ways and of our place in the web of life. I never got pleasure out of taking a life, but I also was conscious that the Creator had put these creatures on the Earth for our subsistence. I never took more than we needed and still don't. I am sad when I hear of those who take fish or game and let them freezer-burn or rot. It is dishonorable.

Mother Earth

There are far too many who do not understand the dependence of human life on the health of the natural environment.

As Indian children, we were taught to respect and see as sacred the connection of all life to Mother Earth, our support system. Mother Earth supports our feet, produces the oxygen we need to breathe and filters the rain that fills the earth's vast underground aquifers.

If it had not been for the stories of Great Auntie that I heard as a boy, I would not be as conscious now of increased pollution and how it is threatening all human life.

I have fished Michigan's waters since I was 6. One of the streams I fished in when I was little was polluted by the septic tanks that ran directly into it from the neighboring homes. It was only later that concern was raised about the stream's rising bacteria levels and the health threat it posed to villagers.

I could not—and still cannot—comprehend the kind of thinking that would allow one to dump waste on roadsides and in lakes and streams, as if the environment would somehow swallow it all and not be altered. The assault on our environment continues unabated.

A few years ago, a scientific research team in a submersible took core samples from Lake Superior's deepest point. It found PCPs, PCBs and mercury in those samples. I wanted to ask how those things got there. What kind of alien would deposit such things in the water that we, as human beings, need to exist? I remember seeing photos of barrels with nuclear waste being dumped in the ocean in the 1950s, knowing that salt water eventually would eat away the metal. Radioactive materials are still dumped on the ocean floor, though now concrete drums are used. Will they last forever?

I fished Lake Superior, and I kept track of the health warnings issued by the Michigan public health department on the lake's fish. I did not want my wife or family to get sick, but I needed the fish to supplement our meals. I was careful when I filleted those fish; I removed the skin and trimmed off the fat—and hoped I had removed most of the contaminants.

There is a manufacturing plant at the head of Keweenaw Bay. The people of the small town there, L'Anse, have become dependent upon the tax base and jobs it provides. The people of L'Anse have compromised their concerns about contamination to the lake because of plant threats to shut down if there are too many complaints.

A few years ago, a man was fishing near one of the drains that runs from the plant into the bay. He noticed a strange odor, and when he cast his lure and reeled it in, the paint on the lure was gone, exposing the bare metal. The fisherman thought the lure defective, so he took it back to the sporting goods store where he had purchased it. The store replaced the lure, and the fisherman went back to where he had been fishing. He cast the lure into the bay, and when he reeled it in, the paint was once again gone!

The same strange odor still permeated the area. The fisherman had a small bottle with a cap that had contained some fruit, so he rinsed out the bottle and took a sample of the water coming out of the drain from the plant. He sent the sample to a state laboratory.

The water sample contained arsenic. The state Department of Environmental Quality was contacted and an investigation began. According to a plant manager, a forklift had ruptured a 55-gallon barrel and its contents had leaked into the drain system and the lake. The company was fined a few hundred dollars for the spill, which it claimed was accidental. Or was it merely convenient? Legally disposing of the arsenic would have cost several thousand dollars.

Recently, water from the plant turned the water in the bay blue. Over the years, the plant also dumped a by-product of its manufacturing processes several hundred yards inland. The state ordered the plant to cover the site with earth and to seed it, to prevent drainage into the lake. It can be seen as an artificial hill containing contaminants that eventually will end up in Lake Superior.

Indian people have been fighting attempts by a mining company to gain access to one of the Upper Peninsula's most pristine wilderness areas. The application for a license to begin mining operations had been tied up in the courts and Michigan Legislature, but it recently was approved by the state Department of Environmental Quality.

The company is interested in the zinc and nickel beneath some sulfur deposits; anyone who has researched the environmental risks of sulfur mining knows that the companies involved in it have very poor track records.

The streams that will be polluted by the mining run into Lake Superior. One federal legislator—who argued in favor of licensing—wrote an article for a local paper after it was obtained, stating that he had been against the project from the beginning.

My sister passed away as a result of cancer a few months ago. Over the years she lived in her home, the quality of her water declined: it had shown higher amounts of strychnine each time it was tested. Now, if homeowners in the area want to sell their property, they are required to put in new wells and install new septic fields. This area was one of the first areas of Michigan where crude oil was extracted from the earth. The underground caverns where the oil had lain for millennia filled with salt brine, a substance that could taint the groundwater—a consequence that apparently was not considered.

Years ago a man fell through the ice on Houghton Lake, downstate in mid-Michigan; the authorities were unable to find his body. That spring, the body washed up onto the shore of Lake Michigan, near Ludington. The body had passed through an underground aquifer.

It seems that the companies that continue to deposit chemicals and manufacturing by-products in or near water are unaware of the threats they are creating for future generations. The automobile—and our massive need for fossil fuels—has damned the Earth.

Now the world is concerned about global warming. Conditions are developing with mild winters and melting glaciers that have never been before. One of our tribal communities in Alaska is being forced to abandon its island home because global warming has reduced the sea ice it needs to survive. The village is now unprotected from fall and winter storms and is literally eroding into the Arctic Ocean. The inhabitants are being forced to abandon the graves of their ancestors and the only home they have ever known due to the unconscionable acts of a civilization that refuses to admit its responsibility and take action.

The Lakotah have a word for these kinds of uncaring, irresponsible people: the word is *Waisichu* (fat-takers). *Waisichu* operate without conscience, without honor, without integrity and without honesty. Their only motive is the accrual of wealth, and to obtain it, they are willing to sacrifice the lives of those who suffer.

Styrofoam and plastic products were designed to reduce the cost of manufacturing and to increase profits. We now have veritable mountains filled with man-made refuse, most of them made up of these non-biodegradable and, in some cases, even toxic, materials. Syringes and plastic packaging litter beaches; plastic refuse is known to cover a Texas-size span of the western Pacific between California and Hawaii.

The list of hazards seems endless.

The exhaust pipes of millions of cars each day leak carbon dioxide and methane into the atmosphere, where they continue to accumulate. Meanwhile, mass transportation—subways and commuter trains—are still only a dream in Michigan and most other states.

The state's majestic old-growth forests are only a dream, too. Today, only two significant remnants exist—Porcupine Mountains Wilderness State Park, the largest virgin forest east of the Mississippi (in the western UP), and the much smaller Hartwick Pines State Park, in the central Lower Peninsula.

Indian people knew there was a certain order to reforestation. We did not mass-cut trees, knowing how the environment would be altered by our actions. We knew the softwoods came up out of the earth first, grew quickly and died. The decaying trees introduced certain enhancements to the soil to encourage the introduction of semi-hardwoods, which lived a little longer. But eventually they, too, died and fell. From their decay and its enhancements the hardwoods grew. The root systems from these hardwoods stabilized the earth and assisted in the filtering process. The shade these big trees provided kept the earth moist and cool. They also produced oxygen from the carbon dioxide we exhaled. Today, we see more and more people carrying oxygen tanks to assist their breathing because of damaged respiratory systems directly related to air pollution.

Michigan was once a vast forest that stretched from Lake Michigan east to Lake Huron, south to Lake Erie and north to Lake Superior. In the 19th century, its gigantic white pines were completely logged off, and in many places red pine and jack pine were introduced because they grew quickly, better suiting logging interests. Red and jack pines seem to generate warmer temperatures under their canopies and are extremely hazardous in the event of a fire, burning so hot that they create their own induction systems. They also alter soil pH levels, making the forest floor much less hospitable to surrounding plants. Growth patterns were disrupted and, in some places, native species were threatened; the environment became more susceptible to invaders.

Today, the graveyards of the UP's original trees are piled with cut logs awaiting transportation to processing plants. The logging interests assure the public they are "farming" trees, selectively cutting only older trees to make way for new ones. But one has only to see the trucks—loaded with logs that are becoming smaller and smaller in diameter—to know that farming has turned to destruction.

There is no part of the environment—groundwater, topsoil, surface water, lake water or the atmosphere—that has not become polluted because of the indifference and avarice of some human beings. And the outer atmosphere is filled with so much space debris that NASA workers now map it to lessen the danger of shuttles being damaged by it!

The last environment to be breached and polluted is the hearts of the men and women who continue to be ignorant or indifferent to the threats. As I write this, the United States has not signed the international treaty to reduce greenhouse gas emissions to slow global warming. It is hard to believe that this refusal is unrelated to U.S. political and financial interests as the world's largest polluter.

It is time to remember Turtle Island—North America—as it was before the Europeans arrived. We Indians maintained a pure and unadulterated environment for thousands of years. We honored Mother Earth so our children and grandchildren and all the generations as yet unborn could live the way we lived. Our carbon footprint was small.

Do today's polluters realize what they are doing to their own descendants? How can they not? Mother Earth, as we Indians so wisely and lovingly refer to the planet, is a living, breathing being. She was created as a part of the universe to ensure the health and well-being of all living things. Her ability to nurture has been severely compromised by unconscionable men and women whose only motivation is to build bigger vaults to contain the wealth they have accrued, stepping over the bodies of those who suffer in the process. So many who do such things declare themselves to be Christians, not realizing that the Landlord of the universe is coming to take possession of His inheritance. He will ask for an account of what has been done to His Garden by those who were assigned to care for it.

I am not a scientist. I am just an Indian, but I know these things and have seen them. I am afraid that the world my grandchildren are growing up in will one day be so polluted that they will not survive.

There is a saying: "The Creator made man upright, but man sought out many inventions." These inventions have polluted the Earth.

Loss

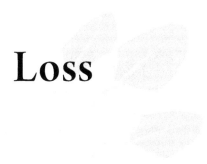

What can I say about our loss—the totality of it—and yet do it in a way that is meaningful to any reader? What can I compare it to in the history of man?

I suppose that any people who have been overrun and forced to comply with an invader's demands would understand what Native Americans have suffered.

Those who have not should try to imagine a population estimated at about 100 million people before the arrival of Europeans—eight to 12 million of them living north of what today is Mexico—being reduced to 200,000 in the United States by 1900.* They should also imagine being disparaged in some 2,000 Hollywood movies as mentally deficient savages and bloodthirsty ravagers of the human beings whose wagon trains rolled in endless waves across their land. Those movies would be translated into six major languages and shipped around the world, distorting the vision of millions more as to who these people really are.

Before the invasion of the Europeans, our land was pure and pristine. The gifts of the Creator surrounded us, and we were happy together. We knew freedom.

But it is not the loss of that freedom that is most tragic; it is the loss of the knowledge of what true freedom really is.

Other Indians sometimes ask me, "Can you destroy a dream like ours?" My response is, "Not as long as there is one of us around who remembers."

It was not just our languages, nations, families and traditions that were lost; it was the knowledge of our natural origins, of how we lived our daily lives in all their seasonal and cultural details and routines. The many attempts to fill that void by the Europeans and later, the U.S. government, have been deeply insulting, painful and tragic. Their languages and traditions were contemptible to us.

I have been privileged to travel to some of the old sacred places that we once knew so intimately on this Earth. There are old trails that are now nearly grown over, yet are still faintly visible.

I would like to walk them all, like Australia's aboriginal people walk their ancient songlines. I would like to fast in every place that we held sacred. I would like to sit in the places where our most honored ancestors gave their lives trying to protect those of us who would follow.

I don't think there are enough days left in my life to allow this, so I live them through the voices of my Red Relations who know each of these places so well.

Our greatest loss is the knowledge of how to walk this Mother Earth and how to pray. We have lost most of our sacred songs, and few of us can sing those that have survived in our native language.

But many of us still know the Seven Grandfather Teachings: *Nbwaakaawin* (Wisdom), *Zaagidwin* (Love), *Mnaadendimowin* (Respect), *Aakwade'ewin* (Bravery), *Gwekwaadiziwin* (Honesty), *Dbaadendiziwin* (Humility) and *Debwewin* (Truth). And I have learned to play the Indian flute and the hand drum; it is a good way to pray and to encourage serenity.

We believe in Seven Generations. The number seven is a sacred number; each one of us contains the blood memory of the seven generations before us. What they knew and experienced is in us. Add to that our own life experiences, and you begin to understand the products that we are.

The Seventh Fire refers to the generation represented by my children, which is believed will reunite each tribe and restore its sense of sovereignty and honor. I pray this will happen.

In many areas we now have tribal language immersion programs, teaching young and old our first language. It is our belief that our language is a spiritual one and that, as we learn to speak it again, we are reviving a consciousness of who we are and renewing our relationship with the Earth and universe. We believe this is essential to our healing and recovery as a people.

At one time I did not like myself. I did not like the brown face or the features that stamped me. I thought that maybe, if I combed my hair a certain way and learned how to speak proper English, I would feel better. The day I admitted to myself that I could not be anything else but Indian was a troubling one. I realized that I would never be considered equal in intelligence, spirituality, career efforts or athletic ability; what was I relegated to?

This life was no life at all. But what was real living? I wanted to know. Wasn't it to be loved by a woman and the children of your union? Wasn't it to be accepted and respected by others? Wasn't it to feel connected with the Creator? Wasn't it to reach a level of total acceptance of one's self?

I think we are promised only today. None of us knows for sure that tomorrow will come—that is in the hand of the Creator. So I decided to live as an Indian and share my gifts.

To be anything else would be to be an impostor. I have been that and I don't like it, and it doesn't like me. I was an impostor because, when I was young, I accepted the interpretations of others, which were based in prejudice and false information. I became an even greater impostor by trying to be what I never could be without abandoning all that I was.

What can I say about our loss in a way that is meaningful to any reader?

I think the magnitude is preserved in a speech by Captain Richard Pratt—the mastermind behind the U.S.

Indian boarding school policy—at the Nineteenth Annual Conference of Charities and Correction in Denver in 1892:

A great general has said that the only good Indian is a dead one, and that high sanction of destruction has been an enormous factor in promoting Indian massacres. In a sense, I agree with the sentiment, but only in this: that all the Indian there is in the race should be dead. Kill the Indian in him, and save the man …

… As we have taken into our national family seven millions of Negroes, and as we receive foreigners at the rate of more than five hundred thousand a year, and assimilate them, it would seem that the time may have arrived when we can very properly make at least the attempt to assimilate our two hundred and fifty thousand Indians, using this proven potent line, and see if that will not end this vexed question and remove them from public attention, where they occupy much more space than they are entitled to either by numbers or worth…

The school at Carlisle is an attempt on the part of the government to do this. Carlisle has always planted treason to the tribe and loyalty to the nation at large … if he gets his living by the sweat of his brow, and demonstrates to the nation that he is a man, he does more good for his race than hundreds of his fellows who cling to their tribal communistic surrounding.

This speech, among thousands of others like it, epitomizes the attitude of the general public in those days and its support for the atmosphere in the boarding schools.

So we search for our survivors; we search for our children; we search for our homes and the way of life we once knew.

We do this despite the continued efforts of the federal government to assimilate us and label us as less than human.

We have traveled a long way in the darkness and have reached the place where we can see the light of day.

I can see it clearly, despite my great anger and sadness over all that has been lost and can never be regained.

I cannot remake my childhood or rewrite my earlier life as an outsider.

But I can live as an Indian. I can share what I have learned with others.

I don't want to just be called *Kikaa Shimauganish* (Elder, Veteran Warrior). I want to have earned the title. I want to walk toward   the light. We Indians walk toward the light, and we will not feign our intentions.

---

*Pre-Columbian population estimates are from *American Holocaust, Columbus and the Conquest of the New World* by historian David Stannard, considered to be the gold standard on the subject. Stannard writes that while debate continues on the exact population, "few informed scholars any longer contend that it was not at least within the range of 75 to 100,000,000 persons, with roughly 8,000,000 to 12,000,000 of them living north of Mexico—while some of the more outstanding scholars in the field have begun to suspect that the true figure was even higher than the highest end of this range." The 200,000 figure—the number of native people that remained in the U.S. in 1990—is from the U.S. Bureau of Indian Affairs.

Hunting

It is early morning. I am watching the light appear on the eastern horizon as the sun announces its arrival and a new day. I am reminded of my Odawa name Biidassige and of the responsibility I have to my people. The darkness of the night giving way to the coming day also reminds me of the many mornings I was in the woods to harvest meat for my family. It was not an effort generated by mental distress because of our need for food, but another opportunity to be close to the Creator.

Most humans cannot see or understand these things because they live surrounded by cement walls, paved streets and steel buildings. The light they see comes from neon signs, yard lights and the lit sidewalks and roads that are illuminated as night approaches. I have been on airplanes at night and have seen large swaths of the continent, and nearly everywhere I looked there were lights. I wonder when it was that people became afraid of the night. I think sometimes that fear makes people sick.

I think the people who know me would consider me a good hunter and provider. That is why I hunted. My children grew up eating venison, fish and other game that I could harvest. When I harvested these species it was important for me to remember that they were gifts to help my family survive. I have never taken a life without feeling some remorse. All life is to be revered, human as well as plant and animal; they are no different.

I learned to put *semma* down and to offer a prayer of thanks for the animal or fish that gave its life so that my family could eat. I think my children are stronger because they ate fish and game that had not been processed and treated with preservatives in some packing plant.

I did not take anything I did not intend to eat. I say this remembering what my father taught me when he bought me a BB-gun. He said, "Don't take anything you are not going to eat." I shot a blue jay one day and tried to hide it. My father's advice was not to be taken lightly, and I believed that my dad would find out; when he got home from work I told him about the blue jay, wondering what it was going to taste like. He did not make me eat it, but it was the last time I shot anything that I did not intend to eat.

There is a natural way to live and an unnatural way that is a danger to mankind. Many people think of certain species as populations to be managed, forgetting that their very presence in the forests and waters enhances and supports life in ways that scientists are just beginning to understand. Man has forgotten that every living thing in the wild represents the natural order of things. To alter any part of the natural environment is to alter one's own life and future. Mankind does not have a management plan that is greater than the Creator's. This has been proven again and again.

It was important to me to start taking my sons with me when they were old enough to hunt. I wanted them to be exposed to the environment the Creator designed for all humans to enjoy. I wanted them to feel what I felt as I watched a sunrise. I wanted them to hear my prayers and to understand why it was important to remember the way of their grandfathers and great-grandfathers, before their own spirits announced their arrival in this life. I wanted them to know that it was not the taking of a life that was so important, but living itself. I wanted them to understand what there was about life that was important to remember and pass on to their own children and grandchildren. I wanted them to understand why these traditions were important to us, knowing it would help them when they became men.

I do not know how many deer I have taken. I abided by the laws of the land most of the time, but there were those times when I was young that my mother, brother and sisters would have gone hungry had it not been for the fish and game that I brought home.

It has always been my belief—and I know, too, the belief of many others—that the Creator provided fish and game for our subsistence and not merely as resources to be financially exploited.

I hope to write more in the future about the game management practices of today. Countless species now present in North America—marine and terrestrial animals, as well as birds, insects, trees and plants—originated on other continents and were introduced here for financial exploitation. The still-increasing number of invasive species is a powerful indicator of the depth of the loss of our consciousness of the Creator's design.

At one time, an estimated 60 million buffalo roamed the plains from Oklahoma to Canada. There was a grass that these buffalo hid in and fed on, called buffalo grass, that grew 10–12 feet high. The federal and European governments encouraged a clothing fashion that could only be met with buffalo hides, and the killing was on. I do not call it hunting. The buffalo carcasses were left to rot in the sun, with no interest in the meat. I have seen pictures of this time, when buffalo bones were piled as high as houses.

Today there are attempts to bring the buffalo back. There are buffalo in parks, where they are artificially protected as panoramic backdrops to the parks' aesthetics. What most people do not realize is that an entire ecosystem was destroyed with the extermination of the buffalo. As these great herds thundered back and forth across the plains, their hooves aerated the earth. Their dung fertilized the ground, allowing buffalo grass to flourish. These great animals provided food and clothing to many of our tribes, and were revered and honored. We could not and still do not understand how anyone could treat them in the manner they were treated. The herds of 60 million buffalo were reduced to less than a thousand. We, native people, identify with the buffalo because we, too, were exterminated. We experienced the same kind of dramatic loss in our population as the buffalo.

Today, many animals used in scientific research also are mistreated and are killed just as indiscriminately. Kept in small cages or pens, they are injected with experimental drugs, which may cause pain and speed their deaths.

In Michigan, I observed one such experiment on a herd of deer kept in a high fenced enclosure. They were injected with chemicals to see what effects the chemicals might have on horn growth and body weight. They died untimely deaths.

To me, the enclosure was a deer prison not unlike the reservations we were forced to live on while the federal government conducted medical experiments on our people.

It grieved me to see this. These animals did not deserve this kind of treatment, but it was another indication to me of how unconscionable this new society had become. There was neither honor in this conduct nor an understanding of what these animals meant to their environment. Animals native to their environment never were meant to be "penned" or "farmed" for meat. Some diseases that are of great concern to conservation biologists originated in "pens" and "farms" like this. Test animals have escaped and spread into the deer population.

I talk to my sons about this as well; it is my prayer and hope that they will never lose sight of what is right about creation and what is wrong with mankind's interference with the balance and harmony the Creator intended in His original design. If my sons will live in this consciousness, their lives will be much better.

My oldest daughter used to go fishing with me; none of my girls were interested in going into the woods with me to hunt. I do not know if this is the way it should be, but it is the way things unfolded. My girls all enjoyed eating the venison, rabbit, partridge, pheasant, squirrel and fish I harvested. I enjoyed watching them fill their bellies, knowing they were not going hungry. They were eating what the Creator gave us to eat, harvested with respect and in gratitude for the Earth's plentitude.

My Heart Attack

I was working for the Michigan Department of Corrections at the time. I had 10 years of seniority, which included recognition of three and one-half of the seven years I served with the Michigan National Guard.

I had given up a lot for the job. We had to move downstate from the Upper Peninsula, and it was heartbreaking to have to leave a part of the state that was not heavily populated for one that was.

I worked my way up from corrections officer to warehouse manager/supervisor, then applied for a lateral transfer after hearing about a new prison opening near Baraga, in the UP. Under a state civil service rule, any facility advertising a vacancy was obligated to favor lateral transfers when hiring new employees. But after interviewing me and promising me the position, the facility's business manager delayed my transfer, hoping that I would become discouraged and withdraw my request. After five months, he realized that I was not going to withdraw my request, and I was hired.

The prison was a maximum security facility, requiring increased security measures even in warehouse operations. Before I arrived there had been an attempt to set up the warehouse to meet the facility's needs, but it was obvious to me that it was grossly inadequate. The acting supervisor had submitted hours of overtime on the project, but I was told that no more overtime would be approved for the reorganization.

The warehouse was responsible for "outfitting" the entire facility with beds, kitchen equipment and desks, in preparation to receive prisoners. When the prisoners started arriving, we also were responsible for issuing toiletries, bedrolls, linens and prison clothing.

As a skilled warehouse supervisor—and because this was a new facility—it was my responsibility to train the warehouse staff members and to write the policies and procedures defining their responsibilities. The staff members, who were called "storekeepers," included employees both inside and outside of the institution; training included working in the inmate store, deliveries, shipping and receiving, inventory control and record-keeping.

I guess I was naïve enough to think that once the warehouse was reorganized and operational, my skills and abilities would be better appreciated and the prison administration would overcome its animosity in being forced to hire me.

The work environment was becoming increasingly hostile. I had storekeepers who did not like taking instructions from an Indian. Some referred to the native flute and drum music I played in my office as "jungle music." The pressure of restructuring and opening a functional warehouse, coupled with the stress of working in a hostile environment, led to a heart attack on October 4, 1993.

Every chance I had to remove myself psychologically and physically from that work environment was relished. I had gone hunting that afternoon in a place called Menge Creek: I had driven to the end of a two-track road, and then walked into the woods to a spot I had picked out where there were signs of a lot of deer. But I had hunted the spot for the previous couple of days and hadn't seen any, so I decided to move farther back into the wilderness.

There were a number of hills that took some effort to climb and descend. I had climbed and descended a couple of these hills when I started feeling nauseated and abnormally short of breath. I was dizzy, and the world was spinning around me; I was so dizzy that I fell down. After resting for a few minutes, I began to feel better and got up to continue my quest. Within 10 steps the conditions returned and I fell down again. The thought crossed my mind that I was having a heart attack and that I needed to get to the main two-track leading down from Baraga Plains to US-41.

It was not long before I was exhausted. There was a light rain falling and I sat down beside a tree, thinking, "This is not a bad place to die." I must have fallen asleep, but when I woke up darkness was settling in, and I could see vehicle headlights as goose hunters came down from the plains on the main two-track. I checked my watch, and it was nearing 7:30 p.m. The two-track was not more than three-quarters of a mile away. Then I could hear my son and my friend, Chill, calling my name from the other side of the swamp. I thought to call out to them but I knew there were sinkholes in that swamp, and I did not want to chance either my son or Chill falling into one of those sinkholes, so I did not answer. I thought the best thing I could do was try to make it to the two-track and possibly get picked up by one of the vehicles coming down from the plains.

I did not know that the Michigan State Police, a search and rescue team and the tribal police were all trying to find me. It was always important to my wife that I tell her where I was going to hunt, just in case such a situation arose. That way, a rescue effort could be focused to a closer proximity than it might otherwise.

It was eventually so dark that I could not see unless a vehicle came through on the main road. I had to feel my way along. I could only take a few steps before feeling nauseated, out of breath and dizzy, which necessitated my sitting down and resting before continuing on. I knew that if I died where I was, the chances of anyone ever finding my body were slim. This weighed on my mind and encouraged me to try to get to the road. At times, it seemed I had covered a considerable distance, but the road still seemed as far away as when I first had seen the headlights. I came to a small stream and followed it to the two-track, where I collapsed. I don't know how long

I lay beside the road before finally seeing headlights approach from the opposite direction the goose hunters had been traveling. It was a state police car.

The officers got out and helped me into the back of their car, and took me to the staging area where the search for me had begun. My wife was waiting. I cried as I held her, because I had thought I would never see her again.

People kept asking me if I was all right. I tried to assure them I was, but then nearly collapsed again. I was rushed to the local hospital emergency room and taken to the intensive care unit. I was medicated and did not know when they hooked me up to all of the machines. I had wires connected to my chest and fluids being injected intravenously.

Early the next morning I felt myself being shaken by a nurse, who called my name over and over again. I asked her why she woke me up, because I had been sleeping so well. She told me that the machines monitoring my heart had flat-lined, and the alarms had gone off, indicating that I was dead. I don't know of a more sobering moment in all my life than that moment. I thought, "Maybe I have not taken my situation as seriously as I should have?"

The medication kept me drugged to the point that all I wanted to do was sleep. I vaguely remember my mother, father and sister coming into the room. My father grabbed my hand and said, "Son, you know this is not right. You are not supposed to leave before we do" (meaning him and Mom).

After a few days of hospital treatment, I was sent home to recuperate. I did not know that the doctor who treated me in emergency and was assigned to my case was under contract to the Michigan Department of Corrections; after eight days of home rest, he released me to go back to work. I could not walk any distance without experiencing some of the symptoms I experienced at the onset of the heart attack. To refuse to return to work was to put my employment in jeopardy. Knowing the hostile conditions I was working under, I did not want to do anything that would encourage the prison administration to fire me. It took me 20 minutes to cross the grounds from the administration building to the warehouse where my office was, 75 yards away. I had no energy or strength.

I started using the Tribal Health Clinic for my medical needs, and visits were scheduled three times a week so that the doctor could check my heart and monitor my blood pressure. I was also directed to a heart specialist who came from the hospital in Marquette: he took some blood samples and sent them to a laboratory.

On my next visit he told me the test results indicated there had been heart damage, and he wanted to schedule me for an angiogram. I knew that this angiogram required me to lay naked on a gurney while a catheter was introduced into an artery in my groin area, leading to my heart. The only women who had seen me naked were my mother, when I was a baby, and my wife. I could not fathom the idea of so many people seeing me lying naked on a gurney during this procedure, so I declined.

In mid-December I woke up early one morning and could not breathe. My chest felt like someone was standing on it. I sat up on the side of the bed and I heard a voice saying, in what sounded like sarcasm, "You are going to die!" The thought came to me that I had not made any preparations concerning what I wanted in the event of my death. So I went downstairs and began writing my "last will and testament."

After writing several pages of information to be given to my wife at my death, I heard her come down the stairs from the bedroom. She asked me what I was doing. When I told her how I was feeling, what I had heard and what I was doing, she tore the papers from my hand and rejected everything. She made an appointment that morning for me to see the doctor. The doctor told me that there was little they could do without the information the angiogram would provide. An appointment was scheduled for the angiogram. My wife called the hospital in Marquette and told them about my modesty issue, and they assured her that most of my body would be covered during the procedure. When we arrived at the hospital my vitals were taken and the blood pressure results were not good. I was taken to a room and preparations were made for the angiogram early the next morning. The hospital had rooms for spouses, so Barb was able to stay.

The angiogram was done with minimal anesthetic. I was awake most of the time, but in a drugged state. I watched the monitor as the catheter with the little camera attached was fed into my artery and projected into my heart. In what seemed like the next moment I was back in my room, forced to lie flat and immobile for four hours. The medicine helped me to do this with little discomfort, and then I was allowed to have my head elevated and take in a little broth.

Six hours after the procedure the heart specialist came into my room, shaking his head. I thought he was shaking his head because he had bad news: The blood tests had indicated there was heart muscle damage, and there had been a question about heart chamber pressures and possible arterial blockage.

I told him to tell me the truth and not to hide anything. He said they could not find anything. The heart chamber pressures were good. There was no heart muscle damage after all, and my arteries were clear! He even went on to say that my cholesterol level was 144. With a puzzled look, he asked, "What do you attribute this all to?" I responded by saying, "Thousands of people praying and a Creator who hears!"

I had learned to fight fear after spending the first part of my life trying to hide from it. I was tired of running and I was tired of capitulating. The hostile conditions in my work environment created fear. I was afraid of losing my job, knowing that some administrations artificially create justifications for terminating employees in callous violation of civil and human rights. The prejudices I experienced at Baraga Max were the same prejudices I had experienced throughout my life. At one time I would have fled, but those days were long past and I decided to stay and fight—and fight I did.

When I returned to work I dictated what I would consider acceptable and unacceptable treatment by storekeepers and other prison employees and officials. I told my immediate supervisor that he was not to refer to me as "Don ho'!" (ho' is prison slang for whore) anymore. I also advised the administration that I was not going to tolerate any treatment that could be defined as prejudiced. Of course, we have all heard the stories about those who have carrots versus those who have sticks: Those in power took my admonition as a direct affront to their authority and began undermining my responsibilities in the warehouse.

For five years I struggled with issues underlying the heart attack, which finally were diagnosed as stress-related. I was given medical leave and referred by my doctor to a Marquette psychiatrist. Dr. Robert Lamb had a good knowledge of the working conditions in the state department of corrections, and had treated a number of state prison employees. He was well versed, and I was fortunate to have him treat me. He recognized my hostile work conditions for what they were— the source of a debilitating anger and rage that could kill— and recommended an extended medical leave. I was given prescriptions to help me sleep and to settle the anxiety I was feeling. Just after I was beginning to take the prescriptions, I received a certified letter from the prison's personnel manager, ordering me to her office under threat of termination if I did not appear at the designated time. Under the influence of sedatives and one other medicine, I went.

At her office she told me to sign a form or lose my job. So I did, unaware that I had signed a 50-week rights waiver. What that meant was that the department would recognize 50 weeks of medical leave, after which I would be terminated.

I was ordered to see a doctor 500 miles away in Southfield, in the Lower Peninsula. He stated that it appeared that I had had disciplinary problems at some of the other state institutions where I had worked. I asked him if he had seen any employee evaluations indicating disciplinary problem, and he replied that he hadn't.

I had taken a hardship transfer from one institution, and the warden there had said he would "get me" wherever I went in the department. At another institution, there had been an unwarranted destruction of state property that was not reported. I reported it, knowing that I could pay a price for my professionalism, and it was now obvious that this doctor was privy to the jaded information in my work record.

I won my workman's compensation case, but lost my job and 17 years' seniority. I entertained the thought of retaliation, but decided against it—I had already suffered too much stress—and I was years getting over the injustice. I went from earning almost $18 an hour to $6.25 at a part-time job. I had lost nearly everything I had worked for, including my marriage.

I heard an Elder say, "I have some things I want to share with you, but I can't right now because you are too angry to hear them right. Come and see me when you are not so angry."

After completing counseling and feeling better, I went back to the Elder, who told me (after hearing about my experience that first morning in ICU), "You passed out into the Spirit world and brought back a gift for the people." He did not define what the gift was.

I can't remember how long it was after this that I received a mysterious, anonymous note by mail. The note said my life was going to take a decidedly different direction from what I had planned.

I think a close encounter with death brings a greater appreciation for life itself. I saw my place in the world from a different perspective. The things I once thought important were no longer so important, and the truly important things had taken their place. I heard the birds sing better and took time to look at flowers. My wife and children became so much more sacred to me.

The extension of this influence included my decision to live as a *Waganakising* Odawa. I was no longer going to try to meet others' expectations or respond to any outside stimuli. The issues I needed to pay attention to were already in me and had been since my birth.

I shed all the Western baggage I could, which included being Democrat or Republican, Protestant or Catholic.

I wanted to live purely, as who I was. I believe the heart attack was the turning point in my life to a better and more conscientious way to live. I am the eldest sibling in my family and, by our traditions, am considered "medicine." I want to be medicine to our people. I could not be this with a false identity or under the influence of an outside agency. I am not Native American or American Indian: I am *Waganakising Odawa*, and that consciousness has made all the difference. I serve the Creator without prejudice. I have experienced a resurgence of life within me. I am a writer, flute player and native artisan. I am writing books and being asked to speak to native and non-native audiences. I recently made my first musical CD at the age of 62, and I am told that it is good.

I could name those who have helped me along the way: These helpers are made up of native and non-native men and women, the many professional and lay people who became advisors and counselors. Their contributions have been enormous. But I do not believe any of this would have happened if it had not been for the change in perspectives and values that took place after my brush with death. I say to the Creator today, I am very grateful.

Brave Native Women

In our culture, it is important to honor Elders and children. But women have performed many of the bravest acts.

A good example arose during the time of the Ghost Dancers* in the 1800s, when our people were struggling to survive and began to dance as a sign of their undying hope. At the time, Indians recorded this story in the form of ledger art. Beautiful Indian drawings and paintings were created in these ledger books they got from missionaries, teachers and traders. Many of the images show Indian women taking an active role in confronting our captors. One shows Indian women riding horses and bravely taking back a sacred pole that had been stolen from our people.

In the ledger art I have seen, women and men seem to move over time from separate circles of daily life—until they move toward unity in this larger effort to preserve our culture. I think in some ways this unification isn't complete, because we still have young men who do not honor women.

One image from the ledger art that stays with me shows a large group of native men and women together, which to me symbolizes the gathering of the nations. That gathering is in my prayer now, and the meaning of Great Auntie's prophecy, "You will find out!" continues to expand.

It has been my good fortune that many brave and loving women have graced my own life. I thank the Creator for every one of them—for my dear mother, Juanita M. Petoskey; for my Great Auntie Ella, who has walked on; for my beloved wife, Barbara, and for my many, many women friends. What follows is what they have to say, in their own words.

My mother asked that this short testimonial be included: "in honor of my son, Warren D. Petoskey, and all of his many accomplishments in life."

I want to offer this in gratitude. He is, has been and always will be a comfort to me—responsible, compassionate and ever mindful of the needs and conditions of my aging life. He and my other children have been role models as caretakers of their parents.

He has overcome unbelievable odds. His own feelings of insecurity and lack of worth, the physical, mental and emotional abuse of an alcohol-addicted father and the racial discrimination of a so-called Christian community all magnified the inner mountains he had to overcome. Through all of this—or because of it—he has always had a strong sense of responsibility for his family, friends, animals and nature.

He possessed a great strength—a genetic gift from both parental lines. From an early age, his far-sighted vision was extraordinary, as was his sense of direction into and out of any type of terrain. He taught himself to play the flute and guitar and, using the strength and agility of his hands, learned to draw and paint. He was always a good vocalist with an inherent sense of rhythm.

Most important of all was his strong connection with his own soul-spirit. As he matured, this spiritual connection with the Creator became an ever-stronger, guiding influence in his life. No matter where he travels he meets people he knows, or makes new friends that he never forgets—nor do they (and he travels a lot).

I am ever grateful for the gift of his presence in my life.

I want to close this by acknowledging the many contributions of my mother to my life. She has continuously encouraged me to think in a healthier, more positive manner. I try to honor her every day, whether I am in her presence or at some distance. She is now living in our home and I consider it a privilege to have her with us. She has represented to me all that a son could hope for in a loving, creative and inspiring soul.

Thank you, Mom.

---

*The Ghost Dance movement began in the 1860s. Indian prophets declared they had seen a vision of Jesus Christ and instructed others on what needed to be done to bring about a new world and free themselves from the invader's harness. As the movement grew, so did concern among the U.S. military. Gen. William Tecumseh Sherman advised Congress and the War Department that unless something was done to quell the movement, the government would have another "Indian problem" on its hands. Sherman was given license to quash the movement at any cost. Reportedly, the last Ghost Dancers were murdered at Wounded Knee in 1890, but the movement went underground and other Ghost Dancers emerged, some relatively recently.

Walk in Grace

My friend Niya was—and is—one of the great gifts the Creator brought my way. She is Lakotah and many will recognize her writing. She walked on in January 2005.

She wrote what follows, though I have given it a title. It speaks of life and love. It speaks of honor and respect. It speaks of forgiveness. There is hardly a day that goes by that I do not think of her and miss her in my life. I know she is not far way.

The Climb

I hurt someone today, and from it a vast revelation came into my life.

I truly had the vision of where it began and where it will go. I thought about my children, about my husband, about his children, and I thought about being alone. I thought about who I am.

I suppose I never really had someone I could rely on. I wondered when this happened in my lifetime. Perhaps, as the daughter of an abuser, I learned very young that it was me against the world. In that resolve, I also found that I never really allowed anyone in. We look at life and keep score so often at what has been done to us. After a while the tally becomes so great that we stop trusting, believing. We become jaded. It becomes a road that is hard-traveled by our own pain. We choose the deep ruts that line the path, and with each one, we travel further, the chasms become wider. We find that some detours did not have to be there.

As I thought deeply, a panorama of my life's experiences rolled before me like the film in a camera. It felt like a death, and no small one at that.

After a few hours I walked to a park by our home. I moved to the little forest area bordering the park and looked up at the sky. I started thinking about how we view age. I saw it as a typical chart that shows birth at the bottom of an inverted "V," middle age at the top and old age at the bottom again.

Suddenly I got a fit of giggling. It had started to rain lightly and there I was, standing in the grass with this huge feeling of wonder. The absurdity of what we do to each other came to me.

Why do we look at life that way? My mind drummed loudly, and suddenly all that was was no more. Answers came to me and in trying to relate it now, I realize nothing will ever be the same.

When we are born we are on the top of the Mountain, we are close to the Great Mystery. We can see all and feel all there is. We look down into the wide and beautiful valley of adulthood and long to know what lies in this peaceful, fertile place. And so it begins. The tumultuous flight to get there and taste life begins to unfold.

We run rambling, tangled in the grasses and vines, as we run headlong down the Mountain. We spin dizzily out of control and keep running downward, tripping and stumbling and collecting things as we tumble headfirst.

We marvel amid the ever-increasing array of things we see and hear and feel. We take some of this and a little of that and add it to our pack. We lose our breath and our innate timing as we hurl faster and farther into the beautiful valley below.

We arrive with scuffed shoes and scraped knees and elbows into the valley of our adulthood, whole and complete and ready to live our lives.

We live. We keep some of what we acquired on our tumble down and discard some as well. We form new ideas and we make new acquaintances that question who and what we are.

This process makes us take stock of where we came from and where we are going. We are forced to decide what is important and what can be left behind. It becomes life—not the life of songs but the life of the spirit that wrote the songs. If we are lucky we get to come to these realizations on our own. If we are luckier, we have not lost those we cared about in the process.

But somewhere amid this process we look up to the West and see another Mountain. This mountain is bigger, more beautiful, and we want to climb it. This Mountain is the second part of life as I see it.

We look back at the fertile valley and back farther at the Mountain from which we sprang, and we know that true life is to climb the Mountain that looms before us now. This Mountain is the lessons we have learned, hopefully leading to a place where there is no longer a need to take score of the wrongs, of the pain.

In this climb we do not freefall and tumble, giddy with life. This climb is slow and methodical. We stop to truly see what we find along the way. We learn to appreciate what is placed before us, and come to understand what life truly is. This climb is long and hard. It takes everything we have to discard old ideas and realize that all the answers were always here, held in trust by the Grandfathers. All we ever needed to do was stop and look and start that long climb.

Each step of this Mountain is a reminder of the People. Their footfalls echo here. Their struggles and pain, their prayers and dreams are alive here, living and breathing. This breath becomes *mita niya*, breath of my spirit.

Their Songs echo into the valley, yet not so many hear them anymore. I hear time. It is my time. The Songs are for those who have left the trials behind them. On this Mountain they are clear and sweet and whole.

I raise my eyes to the summit, capped in snow. I know they are there. I can hear them breathing, swaying to the songs long forgotten, as praying. We are praying, we are praying.

Each step on this path is harder than the one before. It is so. Yet I know within my Heart of Hearts that I will get there, that I will make this climb. I will make it for me, and I will make it for my family. I will climb for the People, and the Children. I will not let my fear of what I cannot control keep my feet from being firmly planted. I will climb until I, too, may be honored to sing with the Old Ones and once again be close to the Great Mystery. I will look back on the valley and the Mountain before it on the other side and smile, and say, "It is good."

"Ni'ye oklhi sni yutakunisni wanzi tu'we yuha wi'hanmna wowihanma iyececa mitawa."

"You cannot destroy one who has dreamed a dream like mine."

A note from the author: I believe the above quote came from Niya's father, who was at Wounded Knee in 1890 as a small child who hid and survived the massacre. Niya's remains are at Wounded Knee now. It is a fitting place for a woman who was arrested in Denver for protesting Columbus Day, went to Sand Creek every year on the anniversary of the massacre and fasted, and was an acquaintance of our dear brother, Leonard Peltier. Niya, I look forward to seeing you again.

Wedded Prejudice

I write this with some apprehension. I think it is relevant to the conditions Barbara and I had to overcome for our relationship to survive as husband and wife.

At the time we met, both of us were drifters. Conditions were present that could have led to neither of us surviving, let alone surviving as husband and wife.

I met Barb in April of 1967. A few weeks later, I wanted my folks to meet her, so I invited her to our house. Barb got to the front lawn but would not go in—she was very shy. I picked her up, over my shoulder, and carried her into the house to meet my parents. Inside, she punched me for all she was worth until I put her down. She tried to compose herself as best she could, flustered by my introduction: "Hey, Paw! Look what I found in the yard. Ain't she pretty! Can I keep her?"

Dad and Mom were both laughing, and if Barb had a reason not to get involved with me, I had given it to her. Later Dad said to me, "If I was you, son, I would marry that girl." Coming from my dad, that was significant approval.

Barb's home situation was such that she was looking for stability and someone who could show real love and caring for her. I was looking for the same thing.

Barb was not yet 16 years of age when I asked her to marry me, in early June of 1967. She told me I would have to go ask her father for his approval, which I did

Her father asked Barb to go for a ride with him, leaving me sitting in the house, waiting for their return. Unless you have been in such a situation, you can't begin to appreciate all of the emotions that were coursing through me. Barbara was like the appearance of a great light in the midst of all my darkness. She had a quiet, unassuming nature and the appearance of an angel. How I loved her!

I expected rejection. I was used to it. I did have an evening-orchid-colored 1965 Chevrolet Impala with a black interior. And I did have a full-time job that paid decent money. But I was an Indian. Her family had not identified themselves as being Native American and talked with an Arkansas accent.

I anxiously awaited Barb and her father's return. When they finally arrived, her father had a stern look on his face, and I know a "sinking" feeling was evident on my face. He took his chair in the front room, turned to me and gave his approval, though not without also making clear his expectations for his daughter's care.

When we announced our engagement, Barb's sister planned a wedding shower for her. Many of her female relatives were missing and their excuse was "Barb is either marrying a nigger or a Mexican!"

Barb's father was still drinking heavily and most of the dysfunctions that went along with such behavior were present in his life. My father had quit drinking a few years earlier and he and Mom wanted to host the wedding in their home. Mom later told me how Dad had gotten decorations with crepe paper and bells and raced around the house, putting them up in anticipation of the wedding. We had a minister come to do the ceremony, and I will always be grateful that Barb would decide to spend her life with me.

It was not long into our marriage before two of Barb's sisters and her brother came to live with us. Barb's dad and I went to the courthouse in Mason, and I was given custody of the younger sister and brother. I never thought about cost or the increased responsibility; I only knew they needed a safe place to live.

It was not too long into our marriage that Barb and I realized that we had brought "baggage" with us from our homes. Some of it was good, such as Barb introducing me to her larger family of Christian believers. But some of it was not. Racism was a major issue in part of Barb's family. While she had overlooked that prejudice and the reaction of some of her family members in choosing to marry me, I felt prejudice around us at every family gathering. I had known enough of it in my life to recognize even its most subtle expressions.

All these years later—Barb and I will soon celebrate our 41st year together—the prejudice seems to have been resolved. Old members of the Curton family have passed on, and most of those who are still living have always treated me well. I don't want to cause any more animosity than what is already present.

I think sometimes that those who acted badly didn't know what they were doing—I don't think they saw themselves in their behaviors. But I had experienced enough prejudice in my life to know what it was, even in its most subtle forms.

These were difficult issues for my wife. She loved her family, even those who exhibited such behaviors, and was torn as to what to do. It hurt me at times when it seemed she defended those who behaved badly. This could have been a major stumbling block in our relationship had we not recognized it and been determined to support each other. In one case, an aunt attacked my people, calling us all lazy heathens and drunkards. She was an aunt by marriage and thought to be a good Christian woman. I was sitting at the table at the time. I stood up and told her that she was the most ignorant woman I had ever met, not because she was prejudiced, but because she had no qualms at expressing her distasteful views in the presence of one of the very people she was castigating.

Barb wasn't with me—I had gone down with her dad to help him paint their home. I didn't stay to help. I asked Barb's dad to take me home or I would hitchhike. I was not going to stay anywhere near that house. Barb was shocked when I got home and told her what had happened.

Perhaps it took the seasoning of these experiences to propel me on in my life. I do not know. But it took a lot of years to get to the place where I could accept these things for what they were, and not entertain the idea of revenge and obsess on the need for retribution.

Barbara's Story

This is from my wife, Barbara, who walks with me always:

A young boy had a dream of the girl he would meet and marry. A young girl of 15 was praying for a man to come into her life and love her for who she was. It is this story that I will try to share with you.

I will start with a short history of my life. This is needed so that you can understand how Warren Donald Petoskey and Barbara Louise Curton's destinies brought them together. "What God has put together, let no man put asunder."

My parents divorced when I was 12. We lived in the small agricultural town of Stockbridge; we had onion and lettuce fields, peppermint stills and farms made up of wheat, corn and beans. A large part of the population was made up of Southerners who moved north for jobs. In the summers, migrant workers came from Texas and Mexico to work the harvest. Warren spent part of his childhood in this town, too. This area is where he learned to enjoy country music and Southern hospitality. This is also where he experienced racial bigotry and prejudice.

After my parents divorced, my mother had a nervous breakdown. My oldest brother and my mother's niece had her placed in a state mental hospital. My three sisters, youngest brother and I went to live with my dad's parents in Pontiac. As most children do, I felt somehow responsible for their divorce, thinking: "If I had been a better kid, helped more around the house, and followed the rules better …"

My grandparents in Pontiac were Born Again Christians. They didn't just go to church; they did their best to live according to the teachings and example of Jesus Christ. This environment had a big impact on us kids. My mom and dad had both quit attending church when I was 3 years old. Dad had been a youth leader in a church in Illinois. He moved his family to Michigan in hopes of making a better life, but in doing so he abandoned God, and the influence of the church was lost in our lives. He eventually fell into alcoholism.

After 10 years away from a church, I was baptized by immersion in water in the name of Jesus Christ. I felt brand-new and was part of a new family in Christ.

My grandmother was not in the best of health, and we were a burden to her. She gave us household chores to do, but caring for us was wearing her out. So my aunt Dorothy asked me to come and live with her when I was 14 years of age. She had two adopted sons and needed a babysitter. I made the mistake of watching TV shows she didn't approve of, and she put me on a bus to go live with my dad and his new wife, back in Stockbridge.

Dad and Mary Lou drank and fought a lot. Mary Lou had a daughter and she was not happy with the sudden increase in family size, which created tension in the house. There was no one to encourage my growth in the faith and before long, I was participating in some of the same activities as my dad and stepmother.

In March of 1967, as I was walking home from school, an evening-orchid-colored Chevy Impala pulled alongside of me. A boy I knew from school asked if I would like a ride home. The driver was a handsome stranger who was in town for his grandfather's funeral. Dwayne introduced me to Warren Donald Petoskey. He was tan, slim, and had the most beautiful green eyes with thick, long eyelashes.

The second time Warren and I met was at my house; my sister had invited Don to a party she was having. He kissed me when we were alone in the kitchen, and our romance ignited. I particularly remember a song by Buck Owens that was popular at the time, *Beware of the Tall Dark Stranger.* This song became my theme song as I thought about this guy who had come into my life.

I loved Don's knowledge of the woods. He took me hiking and taught me about berries. He showed me the beautiful white trillium flowers and how to spot morel mushrooms in spring. He showed me deer rubs, their runs and how to identify their bedding areas. He sang love songs and ballads to me and recited poetry. I loved our days fishing on South Lake. He taught me how to bait a hook, catch a fish and take the fish off the hook. I loved watching him row a boat—his strong arms and powerful chest working together in a steady rhythm—and the boat's response. He would point out wildlife to me and I could sense his great respect for God's creation. He taught me a respect for these things that I had never known.

We had been dating for about a month or so when he asked me to wear his ring. I was thrilled and welcomed the opportunity. When we rode into town, boys that used to harass me with catcalls now turned their faces away. Don was my hero and protector.

He loved speed, and our first fight was in his car. We had gone for a ride and were on our way back to town when he told me his car would do 120 miles an hour. I didn't believe him, so he showed me. I became scared and yelled at him to stop and let me out. He took me home and didn't come by the next day, but he did show up the day after that, the car race forgotten.

One evening after bringing me home from a drive, I suggested he take his ring back, feeling that we were moving too fast. I thought we needed to date others to make sure of our commitment. He looked me in the face and said he was already sure. I asked him if I would see him again, and he said if I gave his ring back I would never see him again, and no boy in this town would ever date me. My 15-year-old heart swelled to think that anyone would care for me that much. I did not give Don his ring back.

Near the end of May, Don asked me to marry him, but he was my first serious boyfriend and I was scared. Looking back, I believe the Lord helped me to know my heart and say yes. Don was the answer to my prayers.

We were married in his parents' living room four days after my 16th birthday. Don had bought me a prom dress. It was white, pretty and suited the occasion. Don's mother made a cake and his dad decorated their house. My dad and stepmother showed up drunk. My mother did not come because the "other" woman was there, but my sisters, brothers and some of our friends attended.

I remember thinking that Don's mother was worried that he was making another mistake. An earlier marriage had ended after two months. Don's first wife cheated on him and he had had the marriage annulled.

Don admitted there were signs the marriage wouldn't last, but he ignored them.

I remember that as I was dressing for the wedding, I wanted to climb out the bathroom window and escape. I was really scared.

A lot of people in town gave the marriage a year, at best. Little did they know the power of the love propelling us. Together we have brought seven children into this world: four daughters and three sons. We enjoy 14 grandchildren and will soon celebrate our 41st year together. I can't say it has been an easy journey. We have made a lot of adjustments over the years.

Some of my family would not come to my bridal shower because they thought I was marrying "a nigger or a Mexican." I am saying this to let you know about some of the handicaps we were facing. After our wedding ceremony, a number of us rode around town, honking our horns. The local police officer pulled us over and said, "Go home! The whole damn town knows!" Don tried to get out of the back window of the two-door car we were riding in, and asked the cop to get out of his; it was all I could do to keep him from punching the officer in the nose.

I was unaware at the time of how much discrimination Don had experienced in his life. I did know of his native ancestry and his love of the Creator and all life. He told me once that he could pray and feel God's presence more powerfully in the woods than in any church. He told me he believed that when he died, he would cross over to the happy hunting grounds the Creator had prepared for him and his people. He promised that if he died first, he would wait for me to cross over, too, and that we would be together forever.

I already believed that Jesus had gone to prepare a place for those who believed in and served Him. But I was so into living and loving this life that I had not shared that faith with Don. It wasn't until our first child, Diana Lynn, was born that I began to seek the Lord's direction in our life.

I had been baptized in water, but had not received the baptism of the Holy Ghost. Diana Lynn was about 18 months old and brought an essence to our marriage that is indescribable. We had a nice apartment in another small farming community about 14 miles from Stockbridge.

Don was a National Guardsman and worked in a federal army depot in Lansing. But he was drinking pretty heavily, and was often off with his buddies. This was causing a lot of problems in our relationship. I was too young to go with him and was left at home to care for our child. The more I complained, the greater the contention between us, which led to Don leaving more often and drinking more heavily. He became the bouncer for a local tavern. I was very lonely and unhappy.

At this time my sister, Judy, who had married Don's brother, Jon, decided she wanted to start going to church again. She wanted the Lord back in her life and she wanted the baptism of the Holy Ghost. She searched the phone book and chose a Pentecostal church in Lansing.

She asked me to go with her. I didn't really want to go, but she insisted. So I went, and at the first service I felt the tug of God's love. On my third trip, I went to the altar and gave myself to the Lord. He filled me with His Spirit and with the ability to speak in tongues. I felt brand-new.

Don saw the change in me immediately. I had a love inside that was pure. Life felt precious and beautiful. I stopped complaining and arguing with Don. When he questioned me, I told him I was living my life for the Lord Jesus Christ. He responded by telling me that I had to stop going to church, or he was going to divorce me. I reiterated my love for Don, but said I loved Jesus more and would pray for him. Later, I found out that Don had told his parents he thought he would have to leave Diana and me. They admonished him to wait and see. What I didn't know at the time was that after we would go to bed and I would drop off to sleep, Don would get down on his knees and ask the Lord to show him the truth: not as man had presented it to him, but as the Creator meant it to be.

We had gone to visit my grandparents in Pontiac when Grandpa asked Don to go to church with him. Don has always exhibited a great respect for the elderly. He told Grandpa he would go, but that no one had better try to make him go to the altar. The service that night was awesome. The Lord began to deal with Don from the very first hymn. Don began to weep—which was completely unlike him in a crowd—as the Spirit of God moved on him.

Grandpa led Don to the minister. The minister asked Don what he could do for him, and Don told him that he needed to be baptized. The Lord was answering our prayers, and He has continued to throughout our years together.

We dedicated our lives to His service, and he blessed us with six more children. Don was called into the ministry to share his experience and revelation. The Lord led us through organized religion in preparation for bringing Don's message to others. When we broke away, it was very painful. We felt cast adrift and lonely.

On a trip home to the Upper Peninsula from downstate, Don announced that the Lord had told him that it was okay to be *Waganakising* Odawa. He stopped going to church, grew his hair out, started burning sage and began doing research on historical trauma. He became obsessed with the subject, as he had with the Bible when he first committed his life to Christ—nobody could meet him without hearing about Jesus. Now it was "historical trauma" and the damage it had done to the lives of native people. Our church family in the UP was concerned about him and didn't know what had changed him. I was scared the research would take him away from the truth.

At one point, I planned to go and stay with my sister, Judy, who had moved with her husband to Connecticut. I thought it would give me the opportunity to pray and sort things out. I was really confused. I knew what Don was saying: The real issues among his people were not being addressed. This new ministry was so different from what we had been taught in other churches. Somehow God gave me the strength to stand by Don and be patient.

I have come to understand what he says and why he says it. I am convinced that the truth will set us all free, and it seems that in this country there is an attempt to keep the populace from knowing the truth. So I have joined Don in his efforts to teach others of the conditions our native people face and the multiple and complex causes of their suffering.

As I have said, we will soon celebrate 41 years of service to each other, Jesus Christ and our family. We continue to make adjustments regarding the changes that come with aging and our work (currently, I work with elementary-school children for Superior AmeriCorps, a division of the Peace Corps).

We have always shared our home either with my siblings or our children, and we recently invited Don's 81-year-old mother to live with us. In our many years of marriage we have had only a few months alone with each other. I still affirm "for better or worse, in sickness and in health, for richer or poorer."

I take you my love, Warren Donald Petoskey.

Note from the author: Barb's great-grandmother and great-grandfather were in the Trail of Tears. But her family never talked about it and she has little, if any, knowledge of it. The fact that she does not mention it is an indication of the impact of historical trauma in her life. We have uncovered some information, but she has not made the connection. She is working on it, but having a difficult time.

Come Follow Me

Chief Frank Fool's Crow said that all he was trying to do was be a "hollow bone" the Creator could speak through. That is all I am trying to do.

Whatever I am today, the only credit I can take is that I gave up control, turning my life over to the Creator. People like what they feel and hear around me, but when I share how I came to be this way and who directs my life, they want to argue.

There is a saying: "When you were young you dressed yourself and went where you chose to, but when you are old another will clothe you and you will go where you would not have otherwise journeyed."

That, in a nutshell, is the story of my life. My consciousness of and connection with the Creator evolved, as it was meant to.

I have said that I unexpectedly was baptized in 1969. Less than two years later, I began my ministry as one of the young ministers who got up at Thursday-night service and exhorted. Another year went by. I did not want to think that I was practicing a real ministry, because I wasn't. I knew that what I had to say fell as far short of its mark as a college graduation address given by a kindergartner, but I was anxious to learn and grow.

Soon, I was invited to minister for three days at a small church. It was my first opportunity to "graduate" from the Thursday-night service and see if I really had anything to offer.

During that period, several people gave their lives to the Lord, confirming my calling. Other pastors started asking me to minister at their churches, and I got busier and more involved.

Barb and I assisted in establishing new churches in two communities near Pontiac. I remember riding in the back of a pickup truck, preaching through a portable PA system in one town and in a park in another. We passed out flyers and found buildings to rent. We did not attend either of the new churches, preferring to remain at our home church in Pontiac, but we often visited.

Later, a new church in Lansing was being established and Barb felt led to go and help. We assisted the pastor for a year and a half, learning and growing through each experience.

Still later, we moved to Pinckney and helped some close friends establish a church in their basement. The church moved to a rented room behind a bar, back to the pastor's basement and into a small church building in Dexter before landing back in the bar building, which was then renovated as a church.

In 1974—three years after I started preaching on Thursday nights—Barb and I went camping in the Upper Peninsula with some members of the Pinckney church. The mother of one of the members invited us to set up camp in her orchard, and we rented the town hall in nearby L'Anse and held services there each evening.

Visitors started coming right away, and Barb and I were "hooked." We saw a need, but we had been taught that if such a move was the Creator's will, He would let the pastor know. So we waited.

For the next three summers, we returned to L'Anse to camp and hold services, and eventually, the Creator did make His will known—a man who had started attending called the pastor in Pinckney, saying the town needed a full-time minister!

In June of 1978 I stopped by the pastor's house and he asked me what I thought of L'Anse. Knowing the time was right, I replied, "I will pack my bags."

Barb and I had three daughters by this time and by August, we were living near our summer camp in the orchard. Not only was I a part of something sacred—establishing a fellowship—but everything I liked to do was within reach: hunting, fishing, wandering through open land without fear of trespassing … freedom.

There were conflicts: The district presbyter of the United Pentecostal Church, Inc. (UPCI) clearly resented my presence in the UP. At a monthly meeting that I was unable to attend because of my job, he commented that he wasn't sure whether L'Anse was "of God or not." Later I found out that I had crossed a line by not asking his permission to be there, but even if I had, it probably wouldn't have mattered.

He was the kind of man whose leadership style was "my way or the highway," and by that time, I was very tired of that attitude, which I had dealt with all my life. I resigned my UPCI ministerial license, but the organization helped the man who replaced me buy a building, and outreach in L'Anse continues today. I remain friends with many of the people within UPCI, and recently some of its churches have asked me to come and teach from the Native American perspective.

I don't believe any of these experiences hindered my efforts to fulfill my purpose on this Earth. My path continued to open like a fresh-cut trail—even if sometimes I had no choice but to step off that trail. I believed that what I longed and searched for would be fulfilled as long as I submitted to the Creator's will.

After leaving UPCI, I became an independent minister so I could do traditional weddings and funeral ceremonies. I was licensed through my home church in Pontiac, which is now in Auburn Hills. We miss it; it's a very diverse church, and very progressive. We still have a lot of friends and relatives there, but we don't get there as often as we would like.

Some might say that, as a Christian serving the Lord Jesus Christ, it should not matter whether I have an ethnic identity or not. I have tried to accept that, but still cannot.

After holding a ministerial license for 17 years, I was invited to visit the district superintendent of another religious organization I was considering joining. We had not been in his home for very long when he said, "There is a question I have always wanted to ask you: How come you Indians can't be Americans like the rest of us?"

As soon as we were able to get away, we left for our home in the Upper Peninsula. When we got there, I looked out at Hog Island and big, blue Lake Michigan from the highway and asked the Creator if it was all right if I was just *Waganakising* Odawa (I had not yet discovered that I was Lakotah as well).

I did not want to be Protestant or Catholic any longer. I remember making my request silently, sharing with Barb what I had asked and telling her the Creator responded, "It is all right!"

It is all right. It took years of processing and throwing out more "baggage," but through the Creator, I have realized my dream of standing in the light. I have become a native artisan, writer and musician, and a presenter and speaker on our history.

I have come to know Jesus Christ as the visible image of the invisible Creator. He heard my prayers when I was small. He saw my plight and answered when I called out to Him. It is my experience and my story. Nothing can change that. I realize this belief does not "fit" in a modern society, but neither do most of my life experiences. I have lived outside the mainstream, but as Robert Frost wrote in his famous poem, "that has made all the difference."

I know I am not where I need to be, but believe that as long as I am honest before the Giver of Life, I will arrive at my appointed destination. I love life, my family and every human being in a way I never could have before. I continue to dance my dream.

My ministry has changed as I have aged and as my education has continued. When it is my time to leave this Earth and walk on, I want to feel that every ounce of creative energy has been spent and my calling fulfilled. If I have done well, others will tell my story for me.

Peace Is

Peace is a baby's breath on your cheek while she sleeps nestled against your chest.

Peace is the warm memories of those who touched your life and went on in their journey.

Peace is knowing who you are and where you come from.

Peace is knowing that it is okay to be who you are.

Peace is the soft breezes that drift by while you are listening to the thrushes sing their evening songs.

Peace is an Elder's voice offering words of wisdom.

Peace is knowing the truth.

Peace is family around you.

Peace is your children celebrating life with you.

Peace is the sound of the drums and the rhythmic bells of the dancers in the dance.

Peace is spending the day with your wife and drinking coffee.

Peace is praying near the council fires in honor of a memory of a time long ago.

Peace is having the memory and dancing in honor of it.

Peace is corn soup and frybread with friends.

Peace is in the snow and the rain.

Peace is hearing the loving voices of grandchildren calling, as only they can, "Grandpa!"

Peace is standing in the presence of the Creator without fear.

Peace is having a grandson come and ask you to help him with his regalia because he wants to dance.

Peace is having the opportunity to hug your mother and father in their old age and say one more time, "I love you!"

Peace is having friends like you to share feelings with and to hear the beautiful words from your hearts.

I am humbled today by all that I have encountered here.

All Things Beautiful

These things are beautiful:

Among all women, my wife;

Our children, each and every one;

My mother's gentle smile;

My father's weathered hands;

Good friends;

Sunrises that have come my way;

Sunsets on the lake;

Thunder in the sky;

A warm fire to sit by;

An early winter morning;

Watching the deer walking in the woods;

Rain on the roof;

Young people's laughter;

A voice of an Elder, giving counsel;

The Presence of *Ki-ji Manito**;

A lost friend regained;

The smell of autumn leaves, and geese calling in flight;

Grandpa's aged voice;

A walk down a country road;

A stranger's friendly greeting;

Chicken frying on the stove;

Good shoes and a pocketknife;

Flannel shirts and old blue jeans;

Grandchildren sitting on my knee;

The Grand Entry of a powwow;

A baby's eyes;

Wildflowers in the woods;

All my Ancestors and relations.

All things beautiful!

Ki-ji Minito means Great Creator. Some say *Chi-Manido* or *Manito*.

The Source

The premise of our tribal traditional teachings is that everything in life is part of a divine plan.

The distances between the sun and Earth and the moon and Earth are evidence of that consciousness. We are just close enough and far enough so that we neither freeze nor burn. At one time, we were more aware of these things. If you share this consciousness, perhaps the rest of this chapter will deepen that, as well as your sense of security.

In finding our place in this creative universe and realizing our own sacredness, we need to consider one all-important question: Is your birth, your arrival at this particular time and place, accidental or intentional? Is your existence merely the result of Mom and Dad doing it, or is it part of a divine plan?

Two cells collided and an embryo came into existence. In that union was encoded your height, the color of your eyes and hair, your shoe size and everything you would need to make this journey. But because you came from creative energy, you have a need to remain connected to that creative energy. We are spiritual beings on a physical journey, trying to balance the increasingly soul-killing demands of 21st-century life with the genetic memory passed down to us by our most ancient ancestors. All of our ancestors were indigenous people somewhere—if not in the Americas, then in Australia or Asia or Europe.

So if our existence at this particular time and place was intended by the Creator, isn't it safe to assume that we are part of a divine or master plan with a specific purpose and direction? In the Americas, there was a time B.E. (before Europeanism) when everyone believed this; more importantly, our lives reflected it. We originated in infinity and are journeying through this physical existence to infinity.

One man in history tried to define infinity by leading us to imagine a sparrow flying the 186,000 miles from the Earth to the moon, around the moon and back again, to circle the Earth and begin the journey all over again; he said that when the friction of the sparrow's wings as it passed the moon wore the moon away, infinity—or eternity—would have just begun.

I thought that was very poetic, but my own understanding of infinity and eternity is that they are immeasurable. It deepens my understanding of the Source, which is without dimension, and causes me to ask if every bird, wildflower, tree, frog, turtle and fish—every animal and plant—is also part of a greater plan. Or are they just ornaments of life?

Mother Teresa, who worked among the poorest of the poor in Calcutta, had this to say of the extreme poverty, disease and suffering she witnessed every day: "I see the unfolding of the intentions of Jesus Christ all around me."

In her commitment, it is my thought that she saw and understood something greater than the conditions that surrounded her. She wasn't interested in "earning" her way to Heaven. She lived the way she did and served humanity out of her own sense of connection and sacredness, even during the long periods when she felt abandoned by God, as was disclosed after her death. I don't think she considered herself superhuman or a saint. She had a powerful connection to the reality beyond the world of things. It is this connection that science and Western civilization continue to reject, carrying humanity farther and farther away from its genetic memory and consciousness of the Source. We either live our lives connected or we encourage disconnection.

Jesus Christ is quoted as saying, "Know you not that I am in the Father and He is in me?" There are many creation stories among us *Anishinaabeg*. But if one believes, as I do, that human beings were created in Christ's image and likeness, we can come to understand that this Great Spirit enrobed Himself in flesh to live among us and mark a path of exit from the many disconnections that would lie ahead.

Why am I here? Is it safe for me to think that I come from a Divine Source? Is it therefore possible that I am divine as well?

I read about the life of Christ, and one of the charges brought against him at his trial was that "He thinks it not robbery to be considered equal with God." The Pharisees judged this blasphemy and wanted this man they thought impudent to be executed.

Was it possible that Christ had a greater consciousness than those around him of his origin and of his connection to the Designer of the Universe? If we are made in the image and likeness of this Great Creator, then can't we acknowledge that we, too, have been part of His master plan from the beginning, long before our arrival in this time and place?

All my life I wanted to feel good for a change! I wanted to feel that I had some value. I wanted to feel something besides depression and lack of self-worth.

I think we all have the same basic needs, and in visiting with thousands of *Anishinaabeg* over the years, I have found that we all struggle with some of the same issues.

The Bible states that, "In the beginning God created the heavens and the earth" and describes each successive day of creation, ending with the Creator's pronouncement, "It is good."

"Good" is part of creational experience, and it should not surprise any of us that feeling good is an integral part of our own sense of well-being.

We have replaced feeling good about our connection with the Source with a meaningless quest for greater and greater career success and more and more material possessions.

How can I feel good when there is so much around me that is bad? I asked myself that question and received this answer: "What are you focusing on every day? Do you see only all that is wrong in your world, or can you see all that is right?"

I once saw an illustration that I have used over and over again in my presentations on the historical and boarding school trauma and syndrome: I hold up a sheet of white paper with a black dot in the center, and ask the audience members what they see. Nearly every response is, "I see a black dot." I then ask why they didn't see all the white paper.

The exercise illustrates that this is what we do in our lives: We have a tendency to focus on all that is wrong rather than all that is good. By encouraging bad feelings, we are enabling our disconnection from the Source and the Creator's pronouncement that "It is good." Feeling bad is the root cause of anxiety, stress, fear, sadness, suspicion, anger and hatred.

Can you identify the kinds of thoughts you have that encourage bad feelings? Have you come to the place where you can say, with conviction, that our lives are a sacred gift from the Creator? When this understanding comes, you will be able to identify all the things that attempt to invade this level of consciousness and resist them. It takes practice. Never stop resisting.

I have not yet reached the place I want to be, but can say that my existence today is far better than it was.

There is a saying: "As a man thinks in his own heart, so he is." What are you thinking, Warren? To create balance and harmony in our lives, we all need to ask ourselves that question, all the time.

There are people in this world looking for occasions to be offended: they live for them, and if they don't come on a regular basis, they create them. These actions create chaos. These people need to win at any cost. They need to be right in all situations, and continuously need to be the center of attention. They do what they need to do, which may adversely affect you. But they cannot crush your spirit. Those things born of spirit cannot be overcome or subdued. Spirit is eternal.

I have always enjoyed music. Music has energy because it is born of spirit, as are words spoken and written. Therefore, TV shows, newspapers, books and magazines have energy because they are spirit-born.

As *Anishinaabeg* we are taught to speak of "spirit, soul and body," whereas the world speaks of "body, soul and spirit," listing "spirit" last and thus least important. Reverse the order and think first of spirit to maintain a sense of sacredness in your life and a connection with the Source. Change the energy in your life by seeking the Source-Spirit and the good in creation.

The Source I originate from is always creating. We all have the ability to summon the power and energy that comes from the Source—or resist it. When we summon the Source-Spirit, we come under its influence and dormant forces come alive. In this relationship, nothing goes wrong.

The Source of all life is always encouraging the epitome of goodness, beauty and recognition of those things we should consider sacred. I knew that I needed to encourage the co-creation of the world by getting closer to the Source. I also knew that in doing this, I no longer attracted those things that were toxic to my existence as Spirit striving to live on a higher plane.

I intend to be at peace with everyone in my life, knowing that every thought not born on that level is separate from the Source. In that separation is my own separation. I am going to conduct simple acts of kindness, offer a smile, a kind word or a gesture that might encourage someone else: Encourage rather than discourage.

I have come to understand what the medical community has discovered through scientific research, which is that every act of kindness directed at someone stimulates his or her immune system and the release of serotonin, which itself stimulates a sense of well-being and feeling good. It has also been discovered that acts of kindness provide the same benefits to the giver, and even to observers. Imagine for a moment the world that could be co-created if every human being committed random acts of kindness everyday, everywhere.

I've read that telescopic and microscopic views only reaffirm the evidence of infinity, whether they are the views of a single microscopic organism or visions of some distant part of the universe.

There is more that I don't understand than I do understand, but it has made more sense to me to reach for the perfection of creation and the Creator's intent than to continually reaffirm dysfunction and disconnection. I refuse to join low-energy people in their feelings and perspectives. My father taught me that if I wanted to be good at something, I needed—and still need—to find teachers and friends who are living examples, and learn from them.

I know I need to come to the place where I respect myself at all times—not in a prideful way, but in humility. I need to come to a place where I trust the wisdom that created me and brought me forth into this period of human history. I need to come to the place where I believe I am whole and perfect just the way I am.

I can't do this if I am disconnected. I come from the Source, who has a great idea of what I am to be. I've stopped judging others. I've come to understand that once I judge them, I negate them. Judging does not encourage one to be what one can be.

I am not better than anyone else, but I am better than I used to be.

I come from the Source of all things to do what I have been designed and called to do. To do this I need to live in my heart and not my head: That is why the traditions of my ancestors are so important to me. My grandfathers and grandmothers had a greater sense of origin and sacred beauty than I, but we come from the same Source.

I was told to live in awe of who I am, of where I am in creation and of my relationship with the Source.

Dad Walks On

In examining my own issues, I began asking my father questions that only he and those like him could answer. My father began working through his issues, too, and we began a father-son relationship that we had never had.

In his old age I hugged his neck often and heard him say, "I love you, son." I was grateful and able to forgive the rest.

My father turned to alcohol at a young age. I remember being beaten unconscious in one session of abuse—abuse that, according to my mother, happened when I was 3. I have attempted to analyze why he singled me out, but have never been successful. On my 18th birthday he gave me a beer saying, "Son, I have given you a hard way to go." It was his first admission of guilt in his treatment of me.

Some say I am the next-generation version of him, and that I sound like him at times. But I inherited more than his voice. I inherited the residual effects of the boarding school experiences that had poisoned both his and his father's childhoods. The more I learned about the boarding schools, the angrier I became. I wanted to retaliate. I also realized that I was not a good father because I had been raised in a dysfunctional home. I was my father's son and my grandfather's grandson. The biblical words "The sins of the father shall be visited upon the sons unto the third and fourth generation" resonated in my soul.

Some ask me what the boarding school residuals really are. I can think of no greater illustration than my own experience and coming to realize that I was one of many who were scarred. We feel we are invalid. We are depressed and oppress one another.

I don't think anyone can understand real oppression and dysfunction if they haven't experienced them in their own lives. So I do not judge my father and neither, I hope, will readers. He overcame both addiction and the effects of historical and boarding school syndrome and sought peace and truth up until the moment he walked on in 2001, at age 79. I was 56 and his eldest son; the loss to the whole family was devastating.

Dad was a hero to me. I loved him and miss him every day. We celebrated Father's Day together for several years and went golfing together before he walked on. We had a good time together. I knew him by his heart and the expressions of his heart.

I loved what I felt when I thought about his ethnicity and all that it represented to me, my mother, my brother and two sisters. He was *Anishinaabe*, and his mannerisms were that of a traditional *Anishinaabe ninni* (man) and *ogiimaa* (headman).

He knew how to revere quietness. He knew when to teach, and taught through actions more than words. He knew how to encourage and discourage. He did not fit anyone's idea of what one should be or should not be. Many did not understand him and, truthfully, he was difficult to get to know intimately because there was always a part of him held in reserve.

He could be soft and then hard when the situation warranted. He was an activist and advocate for the people, especially for the Little Traverse Bay Band of Odawas.

Dad was independent in most ways, but he was totally dependent when it came to my mother, his children, his 16 grandchildren and his 22 great-grandchildren. He enjoyed privacy and knew how to use it, but he also enjoyed social interaction and meeting new people. He could talk to anyone and encouraged friendship, as was evident by the large diversity of people who attended the memorial service in celebration of his life.

The Lord and my father decided the day and hour he would leave us. He did it as he had done so many other things in his life, understanding his passing to be a private and a sacred affair. He made sure he was alone and left, having said everything he needed to the day before. He wouldn't want me to make an idol of him, and I won't. He has come to me in dreams and we have spoken of many important things. The best thing I can do is to walk the path the Creator has revealed to me and build on the achievements of his activism and advocacy.

Dad, thank you for letting me follow my dreams and make my own mistakes. Thank you for defending me when I felt so alone and betrayed. Thank you for providing a sanctuary and a shoulder I could rest my head and cry on when I wanted to. Thank you for forgiving me when I hurt you. Thank you for singing to me and praying for me. I can recall the music and the blending of our voices anytime I want.

When I put on the silver concho you gave me, I hear you say, "Remember when you wear this in your regalia I will always be dancing with you." You and Great-great-great-grandfather Neias are both beads in my story belt and songs that I sing.

I will always love being asked "You're Warren's son, aren't you?" I feel honored and know a day will come when the last Elder of your generation will have walked on, and no one will ever again ask me that question.

But there are other chapters to be written and an eternity to share together. Warren Frank Petoskey, I know you are not far away, and that brings great comfort. I will embrace our family as you did, and together we will revere your memory and do our best to honor you through our own lives. We will love more and give more and do more. We will gather around Mom and hold her for you and share our marvelous memories of you.

I love you, Dad, as I always have.

The City of Petoskey

The City of Petoskey was named after my great-great-grandfather, Ignatius Petoskey, whose Odawa name was Biidassige, meaning "Early Morning Light" or "One Who Brings the Light."

I have already written about his refusal to send his children to a Catholic boarding school, his creation of a sanctuary for other Odawa who felt as he did, his leadership abilities and the loss of most of his land to European settlers.

Grandfather Biidassige was born in 1797. In 1893 the name of the Odawa village *Mukwa Sebing* was changed to Petoskey through the efforts of the village postmaster, whose job Grandfather Biidassige had held for many years. A year later, Grandfather Biidassige walked on at 97.

A few years ago, an Elder came to me and asked me to accompany him: He took me to a piece of property that had been sold to a developer. I followed him to a place along the Lake Michigan shore, where he pointed out a stone fire ring. It marked the spot where Grandfather Biidassige's wigwam stood before he came down the bay to *Mukwa Sebing*.

It was a moving experience for me. We were given permission to remove the stone fire ring, and reconstructed it on our tribal ceremonial grounds.

At the site of Grandfather Biidassige's wigwam, I sat on a rock where he must have spent a thousand evenings watching the sunset on the bay and offering his prayers. I felt deep grief and loss but also gratefulness that I could, for a few moments, stand in this place where my great-great-grandfather had made his home.

I was able to take two of my sons to the site before the stones were removed, and for that I am grateful, too. I wanted them not only to see the remains of the fire ring, but to experience some of the same emotions that I did. It is one of my missions in life to pass on the consciousness of what it means to be *Waganakising* Odawa. We must be connected to our past in order to have a good future.

In 2001, the year my father died, we held a historical trauma conference in Petoskey. The presenters were both Lakotah and were nationally known for their professional abilities and advocacy regarding the many sources of historical trauma. I helped organize the conference and at the end, after I had spoken about my own history, one of the presenters, Willie Wolf, looked out at the city's landmark water tower, emblazoned in large letters with the name Petoskey, and said: "I will bet you that that water tower represents historical trauma to you."

"It does," I said.

There are many people living in the area now who are caught up in the romanticism of the "City of a Thousand Sunsets," and are charmed by the idea that Indians once lived in the area. Most think we are extinct, even though we still walk among them. But we are disappearing day by day, through assimilation into mainstream culture. So many of our people put on western clothing and act like citizens of the United States, or simply don't know who they are or remember the proud and peaceful nation of their ancestors.

I resist that influence with all that is within me. I pray the day does not come when all we are is a bunch of dusty pictures on museum walls and mere fodder for Western romanticism.

It is important to forgive. I won't say we can forget, but we can forgive. The greatest sense of forgiveness will be realized when church organizations and the U.S. government step forward and help us provide holistic treatment for our people. Maybe they cannot all heal and recover, but we can at least try to reach those who need it most. How we survive as individuals, families and tribes will be determined by how we address these issues.

Making Music

It has been difficult to be happy. So much has been lost and can never be recovered. But I am a blessed man.

It is said if a man dies and has three good friends he is rich, and I have so many more than that. It deepens my faith in the Creator's promise "good measure, pressed down and running over."

I grew up with music. My mother played the piano and she and my father sang together. I remember waking in the morning and hearing her as she played the piano, thinking she was an angel.

My mother is a classical pianist and has always been a little troubled by my interest in country music, especially bluegrass. I could play bits and pieces of music on the piano, but really never wanted to learn to play. I always was drawn to the guitar, and later to the native flute.

One wonders why things happen the way that they do. A couple my wife and I knew had a guitar; the husband had bought it for his wife, but she wasn't interested in playing it, so they sold the guitar to me. I didn't know a single chord, but I bought a chord book and started learning what I could on my own. I taught myself finger-picking and eventually could play basic chords, along with Johnny Cash songs.

I wrote a couple of songs for the guitar years ago, but lost them somewhere in the jungle of papers in boxes in our home. I started playing the guitar occasionally after tribal presentations and, at one presentation, someone in the audience asked if I had a CD with the songs on it. I had never thought of making one. Later, I mentioned the request at a church downstate in Gaylord where I had, at one time, sung the lead in the choir. A man came up and offered his services: He owned a recording studio and said he would help me produce a CD, and that I could pay as I went.

I began praying about this. Over the next several months I thought about making a conventional gospel CD, but I wasn't comfortable with the idea. Then I had another idea.

I often play the guitar and sing, making up lyrics as I go. I was scheduled to do a presentation at an Indian organization in Detroit, and decided to "test" one of my songs at the end of the event. If it was well received, I decided, I would write a few more songs.

I was, and I asked the man who owned the studio to help me make a CD.

As accompaniment, I used a hand drum, flute, guitar, deer horns and dance bells. We prayed before we began recording, smudging down the area by burning sage before each session, and "Medicine for the Ages" came into being.

The first copy was sent to me in Oklahoma, where I was attending an Indian Child Welfare Conference. No one had a CD player, so I couldn't play it! I arrived home too late on a Friday night to play it, and so on Saturday morning, while we were eating breakfast, my mother, my wife and I played the CD—and we all cried. I cried because I wanted it to be something more than just another run-of-the-mill musical expression: I wanted it to elicit true feeling and encourage spiritual connection. We did feel it, but you will have to be the judge if you are ever able to hear it. There are 13 cuts. I would like to end the book with the lyrics to three of them.

—*Dancing My Dream, Biidassige* (Warren Petoskey)

Walking This Road

I've been walking this road a long time

This Red Road, vague by design

Wondering when I will find

My Nation, People and my home

Our prayers, the thoughts in our minds

Searching for faces that are kind

Struggling on in our loss and pain

What will our tomorrows bring

Walking this Red Road home.

Walking this Red Road home.

Shadow Dancers

Shadow dancers moving in time

Hear their chants on the wind

To the places where they send

Shadow dancers moving in line

Shadow dancers dancing in time

The big drum sounds on the earth

Red hearts drawn away

Shadow dancers sing your songs

The Red Road Walk

The Ghost Dance sway

Stories from old times

In languages of ancient rhyme

Ringing in our hearts

From the Shadow land

The Ghost Dance sway

From the Shadow land

The Ghost Dance way

Shadows on the Hills

Shadows on the hills

At the breaking of a new day

In night dreams we dreamt

Thinking of these things

Of the breaking of a new day

The Creator's Light is bright

Touching every man

Reminding us of His Way

It's the breaking of a new day

See the shadows on the hills

See the shadows on the hills

We will sing our songs now

Announcing the new day coming

Looking for the Creator's return

It's the breaking of a new day

See the shadows on the hills

It's the breaking of a new day

About the Author

Warren Donald Petoskey, 63, is an Elder of the *Waganakising* Odawa and *Minneconjou* Lakotah Nations. He is a freelance writer, native artisan, traditional musician and dancer, ordained Christian minister and a lecturer who speaks frequently on the history of the nation's infamous Indian boarding school system. He and his wife, Barbara, live on the Keweenaw Bay Indian Reservation in Michigan's Upper Peninsula. They have seven children and 14 grandchildren.

Warren Petoskey

Warren with father and grandfather

Biidissage (Ignatius Petoskey)

Colophon

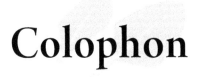

T his book was produced using methods that separate content from presentation. Doing so increases the flexibility and accessibility of the content and allows us to generate editions in different presentation formats quickly and easily.

The content is stored in a standard XML format called DocBook 5 (www.DocBook.org). Adobe InDesign®, the Oxygen® XML Editor and Microsoft Word® were used in the production.

- The print edition is set in Adobe Arno Pro type.
- Cover art and design are by Rick Nease (www.RickNease.com).
- Editing by Pat Chargot.
- Copy editing and styling by Javan Kienzle and Stephanie Fenton.
- Digital encoding and print layout by John Hile.